MAXAVA PRODUCTS & SERVICES

MAXAVA IS A WORLDWIDE PROVIDER OF INNOVATIVE HIGH AVAILABILITY/DISASTER RECOVERY AND MONITORING SOFTWARE SOLUTIONS AND SERVICES FOR THE IBM i PLATFORM.

1 HA SOFTWARE LICENSE

For the DIY crowd, the Maxava software solution eliminates data loss and minimizes downtime in any IBM i environment. This No Data Loss solution replicates all transactions in-sequence as they occur, removing the possibility of synchronization-related locks, hold and waits on the DR server.

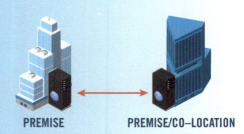

PREMISE   PREMISE/CO–LOCATION

2 HA CLOUD SERVICES (DRaaS)

Looking to reduce CAPEX hardware costs? Maxava DRaaS (Disaster Recovery as a Service) delivers a fully managed & monitored DR service, including software and hosted Cloud infrastructure, for a predictable monthly OPEX fee. So even in the event of a regional disaster, no data is lost and your critical processes stay up and running in the Cloud.

PREMISE   **PRIVATE LPAR**
MULTI-TENANT INFRASTRUCTURE

3 HA CLOUD VAULTING SERVICES (DRaaS-RTV)

For SMB customers on a budget, Maxava DRaaS-RTV (Real-Time Vaulting) can provide the same No Data Loss Cloud option, but with a recovery time similar to traditional vaulting. For an aggressive monthly fee, your production is back up in 48-72 hours, but there is no need to re-key any data resulting from lost transactions.

BACKUP TAPE   RECOVERY TAPE

PREMISE   **PRIVATE LPAR**
MULTI-TENANT INFRASTRUCTURE

4 MAXAVA MONITOR

Maxava Cloud Monitor provides the flexibility to monitor your total IBM i environment anytime, anywhere, by providing a full array of real-time alert notifications. This intuitive interface allows you to monitor and manage your critical operations at home, on the road and in the Cloud.

CONTACT US

Americas • Toll Free 888 400 1541 • nala.sales@maxava.com
UK, Europe, Middle East, Africa • +44 345 557 5705 • emea.sales@maxava.com
Asia, Pacific, Australia, New Zealand • +64 4 801 0140 • ap.sales@maxava.com
Japan • + 81 3 6278 7843 • jp.sales@maxava.com

MAXAVA
MAXIMUM AVAILABILITY

maxava.com

MLP-14002-V1

INTRODUCTION

Thank you for taking time to read the DR Strategy Guide for IBM i, brought to you by WMCPA and Maxava. If you or your team are responsible for the ongoing health and protection of your IBM i systems and data, this guide is designed just for you!

Wisconsin Midrange Computer Professional Association was originally founded in the 80's and has been providing continuous educational opportunities for midrange professionals, to encourage and promote networking opportunities for member organizations. Membership is open to any person, company, group or organization with an interest in midrange systems. WMCPA serves the Midwest business community of Wisconsin, Illinois, Indiana, Michigan, Missouri, Iowa, and Minnesota at our annual Spring Technical Conference.

We are pleased to be able to provide you with this DR Strategy Guide for IBM i. The Guide focuses on the practical tools to implement Disaster Recovery in your IBM i environment. It will demonstrate the best practices for preparing your IBM i environment in the sudden event of an unexpected disaster scenario, and will help you understand the fundamentals of protecting your data, your business and your reputation. This latest edition DR Strategy Guide for IBM i includes comprehensive coverage of Cloud services options and guidelines for building an effective DR strategy!

WMCPA's partnership with Maxava ensures that we can provide you with expert advice and enterprise strength HA/DR solutions using the Maxava HA Suite of products. Maxava solutions are built for the most demanding environments and are designed to support all applications across all industry sectors that run on IBM iOS.

To discuss the contents of this Guide further, or to speak to us about your specific DR requirements, please send email to president@wmcpa.org.

Kind regards,

wmcpa.org

About the WMCPA Annual Spring Technical Conference

In March, we hold our annual 3 day Spring Technical Conference, which is chock full of relevant technical sessions and hands on labs presented by well known industry experts. Our last conference had over 50 sessions and included labs on mobile applications development using supplied tablets. Our conference is located at beautiful Lake Lawn Resort and Conference Center in Delavan, Wisconsin to get the attendees away from the work environment where they can focus on learning.

ABOUT MAXAVA

Maxava is a premier global provider of innovative High Availability and Disaster Recovery software solutions and services for the IBM i platform operating primarily in North America, Europe, Australia/NZ, Japan and Asia.

For over 15 years, the organization's solutions have ensured business resiliency for the world's most demanding IBM i customers via a channel of white-label SaaS, Cloud, Subscription and traditional License revenue generation models.

Maxava can boast over 2,000 installations globally and provides 24x7x365 support directly to over 40 countries through regional offices located in North America, Europe, and Asia Pacific.

Maxava's key technical advantages derive from superior performance and operational ease of use. No IBM i environment is too large, too complex – or too small – to gain significant benefits from real-time replication. Early recognition of the potential of the "Cloud" has seen Maxava committing significant investment to developing specific and comprehensive support for IBM i Cloud-based Business Continuity solutions since 2007. As a result, Maxava HA continues to be at the forefront of the market.

Maxava HA can replicate data and objects in real-time to any number of IBM i systems, regardless of location. Whether the backup server is in the same building, across town, in-state or in another country, Maxava HA can replicate the database to a remote location of choice, ensuring complete data security.

- Designed for the most challenging IBM i environments
- Accessible to user organizations of all sizes
- Extreme performance
- Easy to use
- Minimum support overhead
- Quality and value
- Data secured up to the last transaction
- Return to business as usual as quickly as possible after failure
- Operation without "backup downtime"

Maxava is an IBM Premier Business Partner and IBM MSP Partner, as well as a leading supporter of the IBM i user community through the Maxava iFoundation. The iFoundation provides generous funding exceeding $50,000 per year to the IBM i User Group Community, to assist with community education and networking programs.

Visit maxavaifoundation.com for more detail.

CONTENTS

DOES YOUR BUSINESS NEED A HIGH AVAILABILITY OR DISASTER RECOVERY SOLUTION?

Assess your business needs and environment –
How prepared are you for DOWNTIME and DATA LOSS?

> "YOU MAY NOT BE ABLE TO CONTROL THE EVENT THAT CAUSES UNPLANNED OUTAGE, BUT YOU CAN CONTROL THE OUTCOME."

Organizations cannot control whether or not they will be affected by a natural disaster, extended power outage or any other unplanned incident. However, they can ensure their business is prepared to respond to and recover from these events with minimal disruption or impact to their customers.

Any type of unplanned downtime disrupts business operations and has the potential to cripple a business if a supporting contingency plan is not in place. So what happens after the worst-case scenario becomes a very real disaster situation? Your business is in crisis. Can you rely on past practices or processes? The IT industry is riddled with numerous failed efforts resulting from monolithic Disaster Recovery implementations.

Disaster Recovery and Business Continuity are organizational imperatives that reduce IT risk. The primary goal of companies with no tolerance for downtime is to achieve a higher level of business continuity, ensuring the IBM i is always available no matter the underlying circumstances. Having a fully tested recovery plan in place can increase your credibility as a reliable company that is able to meet service and support commitments following a disaster – giving you a competitive advantage.

Definitions of a Disaster

The textbook definition of a disaster and the direct impact on IT service delivery capabilities is "A sudden, unplanned event that causes great damage and loss to an organization." It's the time factor that determines whether the interruption in IT service delivery is an incident or a disaster. This time factor or business tolerance varies from organization to organization.

AVERAGE NUMBER OF ACTUAL DISRUPTIONS OVER A 24-MONTH GIVEN PERIOD (HOURS)

Human Error
9.5

IT System Failure
5.5

Third-Party Security Failure
5.4

Cyber Security Breach
4.2

Natural or Man-Made Disasters
1.9

Source: Forbes

A commercial definition for "what is a disaster?" is more precise, "anything that stops your business from functioning and that cannot be corrected within an acceptable amount of time to your customers". Disasters are defined and quantified *in time*.

When an interruption occurs there is an immediate need to evaluate what the potential impact may or may not be. The overall outage duration caused by the interruption plays a role in defining the event as either a disaster or merely a disruption in IT service delivery. So, bottom line is that a disaster is defined as any interruption of mission-critical business process for an unacceptable period of time.

This time-related definition reflects the very nature of a disaster and avoids the problems that frequently arise by only applying categorical adjectives to a disaster. Everyone must take a holistic approach to examining what constitutes a disaster, and examine the business and regulatory impacts to your specific organization.

There is no country, state or city that is immune from disaster, although vulnerability to disasters varies. To categorize the threat, there are four types of disaster that are critical to consider when developing your Disaster Recovery plan. While natural or political disasters typically attract the most publicity, they are the least common.

Natural Disasters

These disasters include floods, hurricanes, snow storms, earthquakes, tsunamis and other severe conditions specific to your location that can have an immediate impact on your business. In addition, these natural disasters do generate secondary levels of risk that typically have longer lasting consequences. The result of secondary impacts can be floods, landslides, fires and so on. Risk can vary based on:

* Geographic location - topography of the area

* Proximity to bodies of water

* Building collapse or outage (non-availability; access denial).

Environmental Disasters

These emergencies include industrial accidents (usually involving hazardous material) and occur where these materials are produced. Hazardous disasters are also spawned by proximity to highways and railways where hazardous waste or combustible products that may be transported.

Some of the key factors impacting these include:

* Airport flight paths

* Wind direction

* Proximity to nuclear power plants or other toxic substances

* Concentration of industry.

Technological or Building Disasters

These disasters cover technology infrastructure within the data center or primary facility. Possible disasters include cable cuts, burst pipes in the primary facility or water damage from other tenants in a shared building, data center environmental and mechanical failures, history of utility company in providing uninterrupted power service, brownouts, and operational equipment or other mechanical failures. Other factors could include:

* Power outages or extended failures

* Proximity to power sources

* Damage to systems or data, e.g., by programming, system errors, computer viruses, commercial espionage.

Political Threats and Disasters

These types of disasters or emergencies involve a breakdown of authority, criminal activity, riots or conflicts on city streets, protests, bomb threats, and attacks on your primary facility. This category includes the impact from acts of war. Potential emergencies also include pandemic crises where there may be an onset of a contagious disease that affects the health of your staff, causing a disruption in services and your business. Impacts could include:

* Terrorism

* Civil disturbances and protests

* Strikes

* Vandalism and theft

* Sabotage

* Disgruntled employees or intruders.

Any kind of disaster can interrupt essential computing services. Disasters have a major and long-lasting economic impact on your business, supply chain, staff, and most importantly, your customers.

Downtime and Data Loss - The Real Impact of Any Disaster

Organizations frequently underestimate the impact of any unplanned downtime, or data loss. Sometimes this just comes down to a mismatch between IT and the business: IT may be working on outdated information or expectations, and the business just assumes that IT has it under control – but no one has checked recently. Another factor is the expectation from outside the business. Businesses may be expected to make data externally accessible 24x7x365. This may even be business critical to external parties.

Tolerance for extended system outages is definitely diminishing and businesses who previously claimed "days" as an acceptable recovery time are now stating the need to recover in just hours.

Take a look at the infographic opposite that is based on data mined from Maxava's own customer base to determine the average data turnover rate of various organizations.

In terms of actual data loss, the greatest consideration for businesses is how the growth of data volumes generally may have affected them.

The impact of losing data is directly related to the amount of data processed each day. You can only recover to your backup from yesterday (or earlier) provided you can recreate all the changes or updates that you've made to your database since then. Many companies critically underestimate the amount of data they process each day, or even each hour.

Gartner reports that **70%** of organizations that have gone down for **96** hours never recovered.

Regional Disasters Highlight the Need for Physical Separation

Challenges of the Past

A business is its data. Without it, the business cannot and will not survive. While most organizations have a plan to minimize data loss and recovery time, recent events have pointed at a glaring hole in the traditional Disaster Recovery plan – it did not account for the impact of a regional disaster.

Recovery has traditionally been considered a purely technical concern, but highly-publicized regional disaster events such as Hurricane Sandy in the USA and the Fukushima Daiichi nuclear disaster in Japan have since transformed Disaster Recovery into a financial responsibility. Suddenly, financial officers globally were awakened to a new reality – the tried and true Disaster Recovery plan that they had been trusting was not effective. That shift is still being felt, as the focus of Disaster Recovery becomes more about prevention than recovery. New terms like Resiliency and Continuity have quickly entered the industry lexicon, all about eliminating downtime and data loss. After all, when an everyday user can recover their smart phone data instantly, why can't a business do the same?

Lessons Learned

The impact of Hurricane Sandy is still being felt today, even outside the United States. It, more than any call for best practice, highlighted the need for organizations operating in densely populated areas to have a remote DR strategy in place. The businesses most heavily impacted were caught off guard because they had expected a disaster to be limited to their building itself; they weren't anticipating a regional outage where staff couldn't work at all, for several days.

Hurricane Sandy truly highlighted how severe a modern regional outage can be. While the impact of the storm might have been forgiven within the region (where power had not been restored to local customers suffering from the same problem) the same could not be said of the remote customers who were not affected personally. And while the remote customers might be sympathetic up to a point, they still had to get on with their business and were not willing to wait a week or two to do so.

HOW MANY TRUCKS OF DATA
A DAY CAN YOU AFFORD TO LOSE?

1

Exactly how big is a gig?

One gigabyte is roughly a truck full of books.

2

So that means a small IBM i site could change 3 trucks of data daily.

3

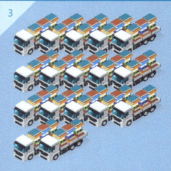

A medium site could turn over 17 trucks.

6

Then we can help you back up your IBM i data On-Premise or to the Cloud in real-time.

5

Maxava can help you figure out your data turnover through our automated discovery process.

4

And a large IBM i site could change over 40 trucks of data every single day!

7

Protect your precious gigabytes, and make disaster recovery easy.

Let Maxava protect your data down to the very last transaction - in the Cloud or On-Premise.

MAXAVA
MAXIMUM AVAILABILITY

maxava.com

11

New Focus

Today's DR focus is risk management, and it is very specific – to survive in a modern economy, an organization must keep its data safely out of harm's way. That is why there is a huge push by market leaders for Business Continuity and Resiliency solutions in the Cloud. Utilizing a remote infrastructure as part of a DR plan safeguards data against large regional disasters, while leveraging remote personnel resources at the same time. This combination ensures that an organization's data is always available to its customers, but without requiring significant investments in additional hardware infrastructure and resources.

Preventative Measures

There is a new saying, that if you can see your backup data center from your office, you are in trouble. The best way to solve a problem is to prevent it from happening in the first place. The call for physical separation does just that, it prevents a problem from even occurring - assuming you leverage real-time replication as part of your new DR plan. This combination of best practice measures ensures that even the highest impact regional disaster will not interrupt your business, because your critical data and the resources needed to continue operations uninterrupted will be instantly available in the worst case scenario.

How Well-Prepared is Your Business for a Disaster?

Over the past ten years the Disaster Recovery and Business Continuity landscape has changed dramatically. Where it was once normal practice to back up IT systems to magnetic tape media on a daily basis, most businesses now recognize that this will expose them to unacceptable downtime and data loss.

The irrecoverable damage of lost data is staggering when you take into account the financial impact of lost revenue, loss of business progress and the cost to recreate both if at all possible. The US Bureau of Labor states that 93% of businesses that experience a significant data loss will be out of business in five years. Companies simply DO NOT financially recover from a disaster when there is no fully documented and tested DR plan integrated into the business.

Disaster Recovery planning will help mitigate risks associated with failure of your primary facility. The most important goal is to enable your company to remain in business. If a disaster strikes, your company has everything to lose.

Disaster Recovery has Evolved – Has Your Business Followed Suit?

Disaster Recovery is your IT department's response to ensuring business continuity. This reaction to a sudden, unplanned event will enable your organization to continue critical business functions until normal IT-related services can resume. Disaster Recovery must address the continuation of critical business operations. Despite the increasing dependence and integration of technology into nearly every aspect of business, most

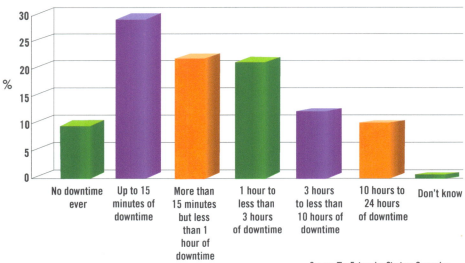

AMOUNT OF DOWNTIME ORGANIZATIONS CAN TOLERATE

Source: The Enterprise Strategy Group, Inc.

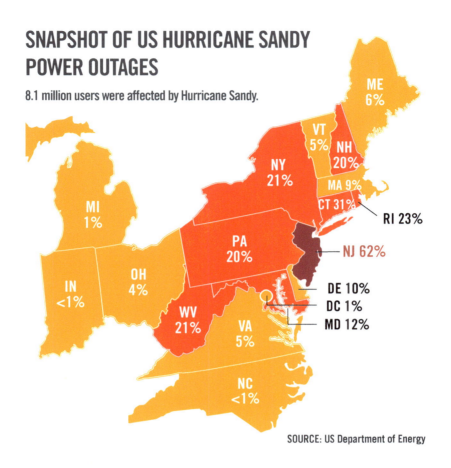

SNAPSHOT OF US HURRICANE SANDY POWER OUTAGES

8.1 million users were affected by Hurricane Sandy.

ME 6%
VT 5%
NH 20%
NY 21%
MA 9%
CT 31%
RI 23%
MI 1%
PA 20%
NJ 62%
IN <1%
OH 4%
DE 10%
DC 1%
MD 12%
WV 21%
VA 5%
NC <1%

SOURCE: US Department of Energy

corporations today remain unprepared to recover IT infrastructure supporting critical business functions in a disaster. By remaining unprepared, you are putting your successful enterprise at risk.

Years, or possibly generations, of corporate value and brand reputation are at risk. You are gambling your corporate future away and hoping a disaster won't strike your organization. Natural or other types of disasters may not have threatened your business directly, but with every news story you may listen to or watch, it should bring the question to mind, "could my business survive that?" Evaluate your company's vulnerability and evaluate its true preparedness.

Insurance can help fund the recovery but it cannot service or replace your valued customers. The difference between failure and success in business depends on how well you're prepared for the unexpected. If a disaster struck today, how would your company do?

It is safe to say that disasters come without warning. Traditional DR planning focuses only on how to restore your servers following a catastrophic site loss of your primary computing facility. This means recovering afterwards from a natural or man-made event or system failure. Tunnel vision does not address the need for continuing operation of your key business processes. While traditional backup and recovery measures remain important, they are far from adequate in meeting today's need for business resiliency in the 21st century. Traditional tape backup and recovery solutions combined with syndicated hotsite providers located without geographic separation are not viable in a regional disaster.

Every organization must examine its risk tolerance to ensure future success in a disaster. These trends and lessons learned from major events such as Tianjin explosions, Super Storm Sandy, Hurricane Irene, the Oklahoma tornadoes, and the earthquakes in Fukushima, Christchurch and Gorkha/Nepal will clearly change the future landscape for recovery. Customer satisfaction is paramount. Trying to obtain new customers or convincing the old ones to hang around in a disaster is an uphill struggle if your corporate image has been damaged.

HOW TO SURVIVE
A DISASTER

Things you need to know about
Disaster Recovery planning

Reasons for Disaster Recovery Planning

A Disaster Recovery plan provides capability to your IT organization to effectively react and mitigate the impact of any disaster-related event. By implementing pre-planned strategies by trained recovery team members, you remove significant risk to your organization. Absence of a Disaster Recovery plan displays a threat to the timely recovery of information assets for your organization as well as possible contravention of legal and compliance requirements.

Whether an unplanned event will impact your systems and result in disaster for your organization, is all about planning.

Business Continuity

Disaster Recovery planning can be defined as planning to ensure continued availability of the services essential to your organization. The definition of essential services will vary by organization: some organizations will see all services as essential, therefore DR planning is not so much about Recovery as about High Availability, i.e., minimizing or even entirely avoiding downtime and data loss.

Disaster Recovery planning prepares an organization to respond to an interruption of essential business functions and provides the guidelines to fully recover these services. A complete and tested Disaster Recovery plan ensures the availability of infrastructure, applications and data, and the IT resources to perform all required actions.

Business Impact

In addition to the traditional concern over lengthy recovery time, recently there has been a much bigger spotlight on data loss. This concern centers around the data lost after a disaster, combined with the inability to capture future transactions.

The average disaster immediately affects IT on two fronts:

- Firstly, the business transactions generated since the last successful and available backup is lost. Some companies still carry a paper trail for every transaction, and can capture these transactions later – causing only temporary data loss. However, most organizations have moved away from paper trails for all transactions. So if an outage occurs and there is no paper trail, then all data generated since your last successful backup is lost. In certain verticals like Healthcare or Banking, the loss of data can cost the organization millions.

- Secondly, access to the system is halted in an outage, preventing staff from working. Even worse, customers are denied access to the service the business is meant to provide. The longer the outage occurs, the more exacerbated the problem becomes until permanent damage is done to the brand.

Business Reputation

The fallout from a disaster can be particularly damaging to a company's brand, as customers unable to access online systems may look for an alternative provider for the required service. While the recovery effort might incur some temporary costs to restore the infrastructure, the damage to a brand can be permanent. Those are the real losses felt by an unprepared organization, and the reason that finance officers are focused on more agile forms of recovery.

Fulfilling Audit Requirements

For years, IT staff viewed the roles of auditors negatively. However, executives have now come to realize the true

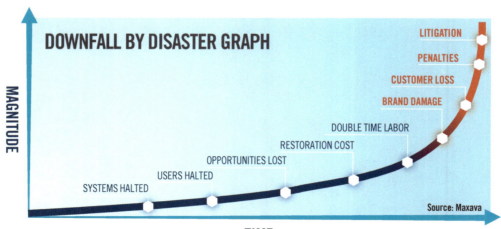

value of an audit. An official audit may come with a formal definition of the acceptable level of disaster preparedness for your organization, and an assessment on how executable your Disaster Recovery plan actually is, i.e., your likelihood of achieving the required level of recovery. Audits have evolved into collaboration rather than confrontation. To protect your company, auditors will review your current disaster preparedness as they assess whether your plan meets acceptable industry recovery practices. Finally, your auditors will verify whether mission-critical applications and data are adequately protected. Auditors will help justify your Disaster Recovery program.

Regulatory Compliance of Disaster Recovery Planning

Meeting this level of compliance requires a multi-step process of identifying and quantifying threats to information technology assets in an effort to demonstrate risk mitigation. In many industries, such as Healthcare, Finance and Utilities, Disaster Recovery planning is required by law and organizational compliance is rigidly enforced. Regulatory compliance adds another layer of complexity within your IT department. Government regulations and compliance rules require that organizations ensure currency, accessibility and retention of their data to predetermined levels.

Being directly affected by a disaster unfortunately is not an acceptable excuse for lack of regulatory compliance. Lawsuits, corporate audits and fines are quickly becoming a harsh reality check for organizations that cannot meet these very high standards.

Publicly traded industries of all types are accountable to Sarbanes-Oxley (SOX) stipulations. SOX compliance has become front and center in organizations today and has been used as the basis for a number of government codes of conduct globally. Anyone doing business with corporations in Canada will be very familiar with the Personal Information Protection and Electronic Documents Act (PIPEDA) which mandates strict controls of access to any form of personal information – a very wide scope. Most countries have or are in the process of developing similar regulations. The risks of non-compliance are serious and include severe fines. Worst case examples have resulted in prosecution of key corporate officers and forced closure.

Securities Commission

Securities Commissions such as the US Securities and Exchange Commission (SEC), the UK Financial Conduct Authority (FCA), the German Federal Financial Supervisory Authority (BaFin) have regulations that mandate the offsite storage and protection of backup

data. If an organization does not meet compliance regulations, the commission will impose fines and keep delinquent companies from doing business on financial exchanges. In the US, the SEC has become very tough, to the extent that new SEC regulations can force your company to lose its ability to trade on the stock exchange.

1.3 HOURS

is the Recovery Time Objective of Best-In-Class Organizations

Source: Sungard
Availability Services

The rules require very strict backup and recovery procedures, documented recovery plans, continuous availability of critical systems, testing, and demonstrating the ability to restore all your data to a consistent and usable state. Your backup and recovery program design will come under scrutiny and every aspect from executing, sign-off, bonded offsite storage, retention and testing, will be reviewed.

Data Protection Acts

Well-known regulations for protection of data are HIPAA (Health Insurance Portability and Accountability Act 1996) in the United States, and DPA (Data Protection Act 1998) in the United Kingdom.

While this type of legislation is aimed more at the protection of privacy than the protection of data, the mandates of HIPAA include segments that deal with Disaster Recovery. HIPAA requires that organizations falling under its regulations take "reasonable" measures to provide Disaster Recovery solutions.

While HIPAA does not specify these measures, it does note that failure to adequately recover from a disaster could lead to non-compliance. Failure to comply inevitably exposes officers of the organization to repercussions, such as fines or imprisonment. Since these organizations must provide DR as part of their HIPAA compliance, the finance department must commit to funding the DR budget.

If you're familiar with any or all of these regulations or terms, then you probably know that you need to look at regulatory compliance as part of your DR planning. In fact, depending on your industry, size, type of business, even your supply chain, you're required to meet certain provisions contained in one or more of these, and maybe other, directives.

Compliance is certainly not a new issue today but has become more stringent and much more complex in recent years.

Framework for an Effective Disaster Recovery Plan

Your organization's Disaster Recovery plan should be a "living document". The plan should be reviewed at regular intervals to ensure it accounts for new applications – both internally-developed and third-party applications such as ERP, and systems added to the IT infrastructure. If necessary, additional data backup and recovery site resources should be implemented as required. Most IT environments are constantly changing, so it's important for your DR plan to develop with these changes and remain current.

As changes occur in any of the areas of your IT environment, these must be incorporated into the plan and distributed as required.

12 Steps to Comprehensive DR Planning

1. Your DR team should be drawn from across the business, defined with roles and responsibilities and contact details.

2. Define your company's different disaster scenarios and the resources required.

3. Understand which business functions are critical to the recovery of the organization for each of the disaster scenarios identified.

4. Understand the key interdependencies between the identified functions and applications.

5. Identify the key IT resources, ensuring there is a proxy or stand-in for each.

6. Understand the systems required for each of the business functions and the key integration points between those systems.

7. Ensure there are detailed infrastructure design documents along with relevant network topology diagrams.

8. Ensure there is sufficient protection for the systems' data: it must be replicated to a backup system on-premise or in the Cloud, and archived to tape or a real-time vault.

9. Ensure that the whereabouts of this backed-up data is documented, and that one or more people on the DR team own this documentation.

10. If a Disaster Recovery partner is contracted to provide data center and workplace relocation, make sure that contact and declaration information is documented and available.

11. Define the process for recovering back to the existing or production site post the disaster.

12. Test, test and retest the Disaster Recovery plan, with all relevant personnel. Your company may one day depend on it.

Criticality of Servers

A hierarchy of all business-critical service offerings and infrastructure to support these applications must be determined through a business impact analysis to identify the scope of your Disaster Recovery plan.

Not all applications and servers that reside in your computer room today are equal in their level of importance to your business. It is important to assign a priority to each business application to ensure that those critical to your organization's business recovery and availability are given more attention. Some applications are real-time, some are batch-transactional and some are simply there for archival purposes – and don't forget email and collaboration applications.

Specifications detailing the minimum recovery requirements for your mission-critical applications are an integral part of any Disaster Recovery plan. These allow you to clearly state your Recovery Point and Recovery Time Objectives, which define the level of resiliency of your business.

Planned Downtime as Part of Your DR Plan

Business operations today are feeling the squeeze. With increased system availability pressures and the importance of data integrity, taking down the production system for any length of time to run backups is no longer feasible. Running backups from the production system can be classed as a frequent, planned outage that can add up to a significant cost! The core business is interrupted during the backup, which in turn can interrupt your users' ability to access your systems, putting your organization at risk of losing those all-important customers.

With business operations so reliant on a comprehensive data backup and recovery strategy, it is vitally important to identify methodologies in your DR Plan that eliminate backup windows and provide effective data protection that will quickly restore business operations in the event of a failure.

This need can be addressed by continuous replication of all critical data between the production and backup systems. The backup process can be moved to the backup system whilst the production system continues to run without interruption to users and customers. With backups being taken from the backup system, all users at all sites will have access to their IBM i data and software applications 24 hours a day, improving business productivity through continuous availability. Continuous or real-time replication as an HA/DR solution is covered in the next chapter.

Satisfy the Need for Testing

Testing is a continuous process. DR testing ranges from simple reviews of the test plan to detailed exercises of your company's ability to restore your computing environments as stated. You should incorporate a variety of tests designed to exercise all components of the plan, staggered throughout the year. Furthermore, you should incorporate the element of surprise into some of these tests. This brings on some sense of realism as true disasters vary in the amount of warning they give you before they actually occur. Potential disasters, such as those that may occur during a data center move, offer a substantial amount of warning. Others, such as power outages or employee sabotage, can occur with no warning at all. Blizzards and hurricanes offer some advance warning but the magnitude and impact is completely unpredictable as weather tracking is an inexact science. All disasters offer some element of surprise, therefore your recovery testing should do the same.

Organizations spend too much time carefully scheduling and project planning to ensure a DR test fits well with everyone's business calendar and they get a perfect result. Disasters almost invariably impact a business on a completely unexpected basis. After a Maxava customer had to recover from a severe earthquake in 2011, their advice to all IT managers was simply "Expect the unexpected!" For this organization, site access restriction was one of the greatest issues.

Passive Testing

Passive testing, also known as a "tabletop exercise" is a scheduled exercise when recovery team members meet in an open forum to discuss required actions for response to a specific business interruption scenario. Every member listed in the Disaster Recovery plan must be present. If your name and role is referenced in the plan, you should be in attendance. Although the tabletop exercise is intended to be informal, it should be structured to ensure discussion, and to explore the procedures, recovery plan detail, information flow and personnel resources assigned to recover critical IT functions. This exercise will validate completeness and accuracy of the plan.

59% of firms were only somewhat successful in meeting recovery objecives during testing

34% are not sure they could respond to a real disaster

Source: Forrester

Prior to scheduling the first desktop exercise, create a realistic disaster scenario. Use a slide deck and review the scenario in point form. Ensure you utilize a realistic scenario. Do your homework on potential disasters for the location involved. Become aware of the types of incidents occurring in your region or country. Passive testing does not exercise the technical procedures or technical actions of the plan. A passive test is a walk-through of the procedures, typically with all the Disaster Recovery team members jointly reading and reviewing the procedures.

The purpose of this exercise is to demonstrate to management and to the recovery team members, that your organization has the ability to resume critical server functions as documented. This familiarization exercise has many positive effects on the recovery team members. The exercise is non-confrontational as the format is conducive to a relaxed environment, which leads to open discussion.

Active Testing

Active tests do not just demonstrate that your Disaster Recovery plans work; they also provide your organization with the opportunity to improve the process and eliminate poor execution. When recovering the business-critical applications as defined in the critical server definitions, time is always of the essence. Minimizing restore times per server is critical. Active testing validates the Disaster Recovery plan in terms of:

1. Recovery capability
2. Completeness
3. Restoration timeline commitments
4. Alternate site configuration
5. Network recovery
6. Offsite records
7. Robustness of plan
8. Opportunities for training

Active testing mandates that the procedures under review be executed exactly as written. Your recovery team should test the procedure for declaring a disaster with your DR solution vendor and support team. If appropriate, test the procedure and the ability of your offsite tape storage provider to deliver backup tape media to the hotsite in a timely manner. Finally, test your recovery methodology for restoring your systems. Each step must be executed completely and the data tested thoroughly by the application owners.

Using an HA/DR Run Book

Once your HA solution is in place, the best mechanism to capture and continuously monitor the activities is a Run Book. Remember your business is always changing, and thousands of transactions are changed, added or deleted each day, so your Run Book should list all items to be monitored and tasks to be performed to ensure business continuity.

Depending on your chosen solution you will have any number of the following to consider:

- Strategies to define
- Backups to maintain
- Tapes to manage
- Networks to manage
- HA software to monitor and manage
- Procedures to update

- Staff resource to train and ensure are always ready to deal with a disaster
- Vendors to manage ensuring the solution is always in line with your organization's needs
- Testing processes to define and implement.

The HA Run Book should address each of these components in detail.

An HA Run Book has four primary functions:

1. It should describe in detail your HA or DR solution, including the scope, objectives and delivery of the architected solution. All assumptions and deliverable milestones need to be clearly outlined in the mission statement. Where applicable, the procedures and schedules specified in this Run Book will detail efficient operation of the DR processes and HA tools to maximize availability in your environment. Failure to adhere to the recommendations listed in the Run Book can cause exposures, or jeopardize availability, resulting in loss of data and/or the unavailability of critical resources to your organization.

2. It must provide detailed procedures for executing the failover process of the architected solution. Dependencies, application and network interfaces, and start-up process should all be clearly outlined to ensure application integrity. This Run Book includes detailed operational, audit, failover, and troubleshooting procedures along with schedules. These are customized to the specifications of your HA/DR solution.

3. The book should contain reference information to assist in invoking, testing and maintaining the solution. This includes the management, monitoring, licensing and backup of the HA architected solution.

4. The owner of the Run Book is responsible for maintaining the procedures and schedules presented to comply with your availability goals and objectives as aligned with your business. This document must always be updated when changes are approved through your change control process, and formally tested to demonstrate success and provide staff training.

A successful Run Book should include:

- HA/DR strategy
- Service level Agreements (SLA to the Business)
- Availability objectives
- RTO (Recovery Time Objective)
- RPO (Recovery Point Objective)
- Roles and responsibilities

- Solution overview
- IBM i and data center server infrastructure architecture details
- Vendor responsibilities
- IBM i application overview
- HA Solution configuration details
- Network information
- Operational (start-up/shutdown)
- Monitoring
- Backups
- IPL procedures
- Planned failover testing procedures
- Unplanned failover/invocation procedures
- Licensing

High Availability Monitoring and Management

Disaster Recovery is a living process where functions should be regularly checked to ensure optimal performance and readiness. Depending on the chosen DR solution, you will use different tools to assist with management and monitoring of the environment:

- Tape backup environments (not strictly a DR solution) rely on limited and manual tools and functions of the IBM i OS that only check parts of the system. IBM's BRMS product offers better management and automation options for tape backup. To verify data written to tape is as expected, lengthy tape catalog processes need to be employed.

- When choosing Data Replication between physical machines for the purposes of Disaster Recovery, monitoring and management tools are provided by the various vendors for other DR environments. Data integrity checking between the production and DR systems is available for most solutions, and regular auditing is highly recommended. In some cases Automated integrity checking and auditing is also available (depending on vendor).

If your DR strategy includes data replication, you will have the opportunity to perform the following Monitoring and management activities:

- Administration
- Alarms and alerts for replication errors
- Alarms and alerts for communication errors
- Replication status

- Integrity and readiness via data sync checks
- Email notification for errors
- IFS and physical file attributes
- New object existence
- Physical file contents
- Triggers
- User spaces
- Development of routines for out-of-sync or suspended objects.

Once your solution is configured, it's important to ensure it is documented. Every HA implementation must be supported with complete and tested procedures detailed in the HA Runbook. Documentation is time-consuming but all this work will pay dividends when put to an executable task. Documentation is key to running successful HA.

Your DR Plan Checklist

Questions for Preparedness

- ☐ Do you have an organization-wide business continuity program that includes a robust Disaster Recovery plan and signed off by the CEO at board level?

- ☐ Is your business continuity and Disaster Recovery plan based upon business impact analysis?

- ☐ Is business continuity and Disaster Recovery included in your corporate risk assessment?

- ☐ Do you have formal agreements for an alternate processing site and equipment should the need arise to relocate operations?

- ☐ Does your Disaster Recovery plan address procedures and priorities for returning to permanent and normal operations?

- ☐ Do you maintain offsite backups of critical information at a sufficiently geographically diverse location from production?

- ☐ Do you have formalized procedures for testing your IT recovery at the data center?

- ☐ Have your business continuity and Disaster Recovery plans been tested in the past six to 12 months?

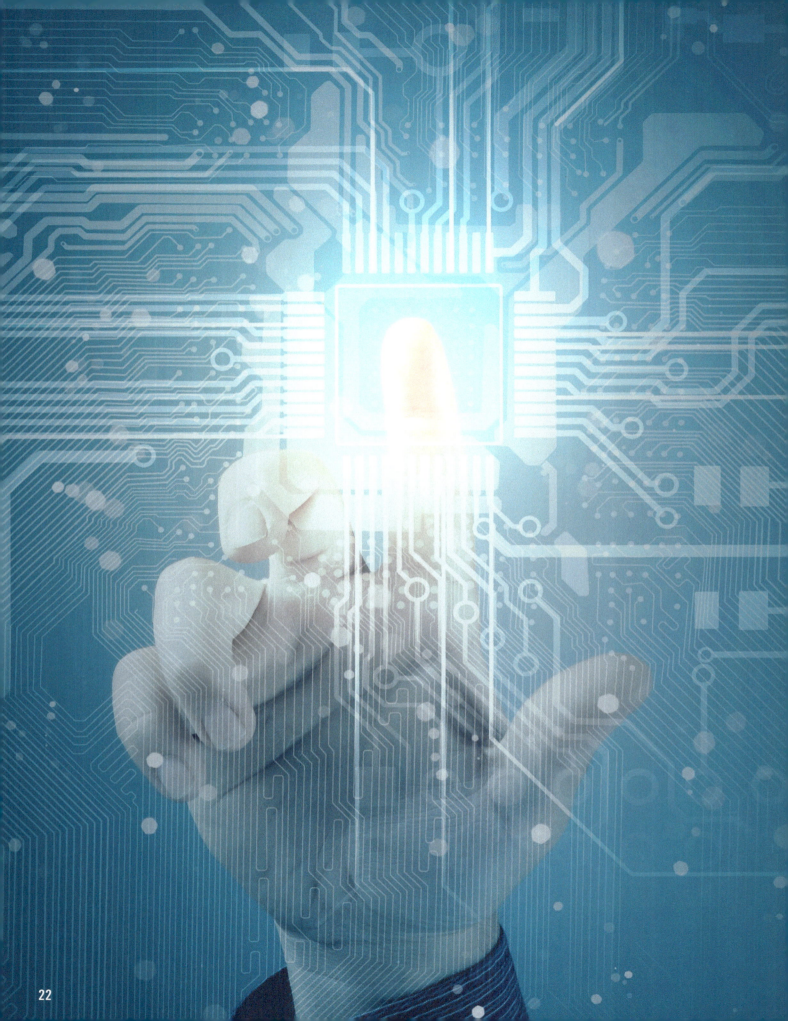

CLOUD OR TRADITIONAL: WHAT DATA PROTECTION AND RECOVERY SOLUTIONS ARE AVAILABLE?

An overview of the HA/DR options available for IBM i

"40% OF LARGE ENTERPRISES WILL HAVE ELIMINATED TAPE FOR OPERATIONAL RECOVERY BY THE END OF 2016 - IBM."

High Availability: Today's Business Requirement

With business today focusing on continuous improvement, IT service delivery is being pressured to reduce capital expenditure and contain costs, while delivering a highly available, resilient and agile IT infrastructure. In this highly demanding environment, IT staff must also demonstrate Disaster Recovery capabilities that meet changing business continuity and compliance requirements. In today's competitive business world, IT services need to strive for availability 24 hours a day, seven days a week.

This is reasonable as it is what the customer demands. Organizations invest considerably in IT infrastructure because they are increasingly reliant on technology to sustain profitability and market share in their business. With technology linked so tightly to everyday business process, the cost of outages is escalating, so enterprises demand shorter downtime windows and quick recovery times for critical applications, with no data loss. Business success is directly linked to continuous and reliable access to that information. E-Business and ERP systems are just two examples where any significant outage will directly affect the enterprise's operations, and revenue - and worse, possibly its very survival.

There is an industry shift from delivering HA strictly for DR (a passive, after-the-fact solution) to business resiliency (system availability all the time). This is due to the fact that most, if not all, stages of the business life-cycle are totally dependent on process delivered by your IT department. If you combine this with dispersed ownership and management (internal and outsourced) of IT services, then providing for business resiliency is a top level concern for enterprises today. Equally vital to business today is maintaining corporate financial stability and business reputation. Infrastructure Services' ability to deliver IBM i systems availability 24x7x365 is typically expressed as a percentage of the total system uptime in a given year. IT typically has agreed with business operations to deliver services through a formal or informal Service Level Agreement (SLA).

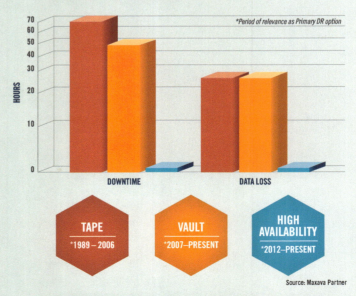

HOURLY LOSS RATE

Source: Maxava Partner

SYSTEMS AVAILABILITY REQUIREMENT

SYSTEMS AVAILABILITY	DOWNTIME PER YEAR	DOWNTIME PER MONTH	DOWNTIME PER WEEK
90% ("one nine")	36.5 days	72 hours	16.8 hours
95%	18.25 days	14.4 hours	8.4 hours
98%	7.30 days	14.4 hours	3.36 hours
99% ("two nines")	3.65 days	7.20 hours	1.68 hours
99.5%	1.83 days	3.60 hours	50.4 minutes
99.9% ("three nines")	8.76 hours	43.2 minutes	10.1 minutes
99.95%	4.38 hours	21.56 minutes	5.04 minutes
99.99% ("four nines")	52.6 minutes	4.32 minutes	1.01 minutes

Source: Wikipedia

All discussions related to systems availability begin with 'the number of nines'. The table below shows the relationship between system availability percentages and the corresponding amount of time your IBM i would be unavailable per year, month or week. Typically, these numbers do not include any planned outages or recovery time from a disaster-related outage. How many 'nines' of uptime can your IT department deliver? Your HA solution needs to help your organization achieve higher systems availability, providing additional system access time to your business.

Tape Backup

The use of magnetic tape media to back up hard disk-based data has been around since the 1960s. Tape has been the backstop for data loss in the event of a catastrophic event or disaster for many years, for many organizations. Although tape is used as a method of archiving data and meeting regulatory compliance, tape backups have several disadvantages:

- Latency — Data volume growth can put pressure on the allocated backup window which in turn is under pressure as businesses strive for increased system availability. Tape-based backups are struggling to keep pace with increased volumes of data, putting Disaster Recovery scenarios at risk that rely solely on tape backup for recovery.

- Unreliability — Tape media failures do occur and can have a significant impact on the recoverability of your business data and by definition, your business.

- Labor-intensive — The tape backup process can

be excessively time-consuming, considering it is a daily requirement.

- Problematic recovery — Recovering data from magnetic tape media is time consuming. There is also a reasonable risk that the data thought to have been backed up isn't actually on the tape due to operator or automation errors. These errors will only be picked up at restoration time and could be detrimental to the recovery of your business data in the case of a serious system failure.

However, there is still a place for tape backup in an organization's data protection plan. When considering data retention policies, tape is an economical solution to long term data retention, so long as the tapes are readable. But the need to achieve reduced RPO and RTO metrics far outstrips the capability of tape and this has led the trend toward logical replication being adopted by small, medium and large businesses alike. The capabilities, operational benefits, scalability and cost benefits of logical replication solutions make them something every IT shop should consider.

Checklist for Tape Backup and Recovery

Organizations using tape backup must consider multiple manual steps to ensure the best recovery possible:

- ☐ Examine current save strategy for all mission-critical servers.

- ☐ Map out how you would rebuild multiple logical partitions (LPARs) or complete IBM i Servers.

- ☐ Consider the bigger picture of enterprise recovery.

- ☐ Check the backup logs for missing objects, folders, directories.
- ☐ Examine backup software: such as BRMS, third-party software solutions, native CL.
- ☐ Are you saving all the required components for both application and system recovery?
- ☐ Review tape management rotations.
- ☐ Review offsite strategies.
- ☐ Model recovery to Recovery Time Objectives.
- ☐ Allow for PTFs and Service Packs.
- ☐ Test and validate alternative IPL functionality.
- ☐ Consider the risk of security issues during recovery.
- ☐ Review all recovery documentation and testing activities.

Vaulting or Offsite Backup

Traditional or Legacy Vaulting

Over the past few years there has been a trend to move from running traditional onsite backups to vaulting or offsite backup solutions. Vaulting involves electronically transmitting the backup data to a secure facility which moves critical data offsite faster than tape couriers. Vaulting can be particularly useful when trying to retrieve a specific file or library – however if the offsite 'vault copy' is to be used for a total Disaster Recovery solution then the same issue exists as for local backups: the recovery point will be limited to the time of the last backup or vault, and this could be up to 24 hours old.

DIY or On-Premise HA Software Replication

What is Software Replication?

Software Replication is also referred to as Logical Replication. IBM i software replication normally utilizes the operating system features of local journaling and remote journaling. Database changes are written to a local journal and replicated to one or many other machines, often over long distances and in real-time.

The Benefits of Software Replication
Over Hardware Replication

The benefits of using software or logical replication include:

- • Ability to set backups to run over on the DR system
- • Transaction updates are still sent to the backup system during the backup process
- • Ability to work with and use the backup copy for reporting and query reporting
- • Ability to exclude not-required objects from replication to reduce overheads
- • With library redirect, you can have multiple source systems replicate to a single backup
- • Ability to roll back transactions via journaling or refresh individual objects where required without the need for a full refresh
- • Ability to replicate over long distances with no impact on the application.

Disadvantages of hardware replication include:

- • If data is updated on the replication target or backup, a full refresh is required to continue replication
- • A database on the backup system is not available for query lookup while being updated
- • It does not replicate the IBM i system ASP
- • No ability to reduce the overhead by excluding unnecessary objects
- • Intolerance for high latency bandwidth.

Checklist For an HA Solution

Traditionally, High Availability on the IBM i was achieved through many different methods, each bringing its own set of challenges. For the highest quality Recovery Time Objective (RTO) and Recovery Point Objective (RPO), the following three main methods are strongly recommended if not mandatory:

- ☐ The architecture behind the replication needs to be 100% based on IBM's Remote Journaling technology. Remote Journaling is IBM's own gold standard for "transmitting journal information between systems". It was created by IBM to be the fastest and most reliable method for replication from one system to another – even in the Cloud.

- ☐ The method for replication must guarantee minimal impact on the production system. This is best achieved by immediately replicating information from the production system over to the backup. This avoids the older methods of filtering, and match-and-merge processes, which can take up extra resources on the production system. There is also no need to use the Security Audit Journal, which should only be used for its intended purpose.

☐ To achieve a Recovery Point Objective of the last transaction processed, the replication process should utilize an architecture that allows for virtually unlimited concurrent apply processes to deliver rapid data replication with no backlog of changes. This process must also leverage functions like Command Intercept to eliminate lag in the processing of data and objects – and more importantly, to avoid both object lock conditions and delays in synchronizing critical data. Using this unique methodology, an organization's systems will always be ready for failover in the event of a disaster. This new approach also makes it possible to run simulated role swap tests on the backup system without having to fail over or swap from production systems as has been required in the past.

HA/DR Options in the Cloud

Why do organizations want Cloud-based HA/DR solutions for IBM i?

HA/DR meets two critical business requirements in event of a disaster:

1. A Recovery Point that is as close to last transaction as possible (Recovery Point Objective or RPO)

2. A return to processing business transactions in as short a timeframe as possible (Recovery Time Objective or RTO).

Typically maintaining an effective HA/DR environment requires:

- The ability to evaluate and select a suitable HA/DR solution

- A remote data center

- A backup IBM i system

- Networking configuration

- Sufficient bandwidth

- HA software

- Technical implementation skills

- Ongoing monitoring and management of the HA environment with skilled personnel.

Fully-hosted Cloud services remove these requirements from a business and provide a "one-stop" solution based on clear contractual terms and agreed SLAs for an inclusive, predictable, monthly fee.

High Availability

High Availability in the Cloud involves sending data in real-time from the customer's primary system to a Cloud provider. The duplicate database is housed in a separate logical partition on a multi-tenanted IBM i machine, often in a professional data center. The logical partition is allocated enough resources to facilitate a full role swap of the customer's users to the Cloud in the event of a disaster at the customer's site. A Cloud HA solution needs to provide a Recovery Point Objective (RPO) of near zero and a Recovery Time Objective (RTO) of less than 1 hour.

Real-Time Vaulting

Real-time vaulting, like HA in the Cloud above, involves sending data in real-time from the customer's primary machine to a Cloud provider. The duplicate database is housed in a separate logical partition on a multi-tenanted IBM i system, often in a professional data center. The difference between the solutions is in the logical partition's resources. The logical partition is allocated enough resources (storage, CPW and memory) for 'replication only' so therefore an immediate role swap is not possible. In the event of a disaster at the customer site, a full copy of the database can be made available on magnetic tape. The customer will avoid any data loss after a disaster and will achieve a Recovery Point Objective (RPO) of near zero. The Recovery Time Objective (RTO) will depend on the customer's Disaster Recovery plan and could be 24 hours or more. Therefore real-time vaulting suits customers who do not have the budget for Cloud HA but want to avoid data loss in a disaster. Customers who require 24x7 recoverability should investigate Cloud HA.

Managed DR Solutions – What is DRaaS and How Does it Work?

In most production data centers today, IT is forced to manage a mixed environment of heterogeneous hardware and software platforms. With IT focused on continuous improvement, IT managers are forced to tighten capital expenditures and contain costs, while delivering a highly available, resilient and agile IT infrastructure. In this highly demanding environment, IT staff must also demonstrate Disaster Recovery capabilities that meet changing demands.

Why do so many traditional DR technologies under-perform and under-deliver? Often the reasons are IT complexity, lack of sufficiently knowledgeable staff and lack of resource in IT infrastructure.

The move to the Cloud has spawned many new concepts of the form 'XXXX as a Service' such as 'Infrastructure as a Service' and 'Software as a Service'.

Fundamentally, DRaaS or Disaster Recovery as a Service is the replication of data from a production data center into the Cloud, i.e., onto systems managed by the Service Provider. These systems can be either physical or virtual machines. The Service Provider can then maintain and monitor the replicated environments, and make them available at the time of test or disaster.

The Cloud solution provided by the MSP as part of a billed service includes: the hardware that the replicated environment resides on; its Operating System and other ancillary software; the transport methods within the Cloud data center; the tools to perform the replication; and the services to monitor and manage the solution.

Can A Cloud DR Strategy Work For You?

Most IT organizations are embracing Cloud solutions as a means to cut costs in their production data centers. But Cloud services are also being adopted for Disaster Recovery as a Service, making for a cost-effective and reliable service offering. By implementing a Cloud-based strategy, you are able to reduce the capital expenditure for your IBM i and decrease complexity, creating significant improvements in the speed and simplicity of your

Disaster Recovery plan. Cloud-based DR can lead to a reduction of the Recovery Time Objective (RTO) for mission-critical applications.

Here are some underlying advantages that Cloud provides when considering your Disaster Recovery requirements:

- Reduced direct costs — The biggest benefit comes from a reduction in upfront capital cost when considering the alternative of buying the DR IBM i outright, and there is no requirement to purchase a separate HA software solution.

- Fixed monthly costs — The customer will normally sign a contract and a Service Level Agreement which includes fixed monthly costs. The fee will be a predictable operational cost.

- Flexible Terms — As this is a Cloud service, negotiating flexible contract terms can be expected.

- Effective hardware utilization — With Cloud solutions the provider has the benefit of scale, utilizing any idle processor cycles along with memory. This translates into reduced cost for the customer.

- Speed of setup — With the Cloud server, an HA backup logical partition can be pre-provisioned with the relevant operating system version, in a ready state for customer consumption.

- Proven recovery — The simplified DR environment

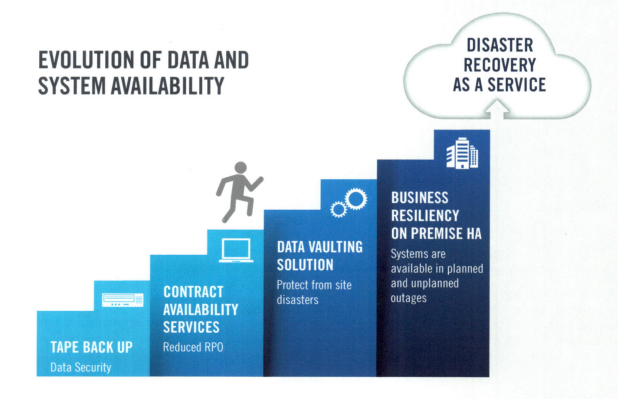

EVOLUTION OF DATA AND SYSTEM AVAILABILITY

DISASTER RECOVERY AS A SERVICE

TAPE BACK UP
Data Security

CONTRACT AVAILABILITY SERVICES
Reduced RPO

DATA VAULTING SOLUTION
Protect from site disasters

BUSINESS RESILIENCY ON PREMISE HA
Systems are available in planned and unplanned outages

THE RIGHT FIT FOR YOUR BUSINESS — CLOUD OR ON-PREMISE?

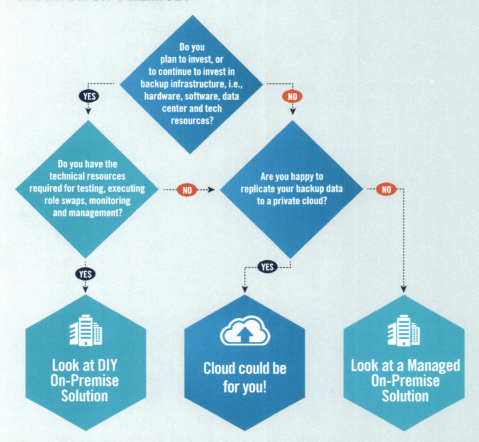

deployment allows for more frequent and thorough testing of the applications. Concluding a successful test, the DR services is immediately available in the case of a disaster.

- Easier manageability — Failover to the DR service is managed by experts, allowing a speedy recovery at a remote location.

- Reduced reliance on knowledgeable staff — Having in-house staff specializing in DR applications is no longer a factor as the right Cloud provider will have the skills to manage the end-to-end solution.

- Handles tighter RPOs and RTOs — Scale is available in the Cloud to improve recovery objectives as business needs justify the cost of HA/DR.

Hybrid, Private and Public Clouds

Hybrid Environments

A hybrid environment extends the availability of an organization's on-premise system by leveraging the use of Cloud Infrastructure as a hot backup system. The use

of the Cloud Infrastructure and its internal network is typically provided by a Managed Service Provider via a fixed monthly rental cost, sometimes with a mix of additional management services.

In the case of DRaaS, an organization's on-premise system is replicated in real-time to a Cloud Infrastructure located in the Cloud, and the software and management of the replication process is included as part of the overall Service. The Cloud Infrastructure is always available in the event of a failover, and can be delivered via two hybrid options: Private or Public. The viability of each is chiefly dependent on the level of data security required.

Private Cloud

In the case of Private Cloud, the Cloud Infrastructure is exclusively for the use of a single organization. This reduces security and compliance risks, as the data is uniquely separated from other organizations managed by the Service Provider. The primary benefit of this hybrid option is that it works just as if an organization had leveraged its own off-premise system internally. The difference here is primarily commercial: to leverage its own system, an organization would have the CAPEX costs associated with a second system, whereas with a Private Cloud, the remote Infrastructure is simply rented on a monthly basis as an OPEX expense.

In a DRaaS model, an organization's on-premise system is replicated in real-time to a private infrastructure in the Cloud. The replication, infrastructure and the management of both are provided by a Service Provider as a fixed monthly cost. This reduces the CAPEX costs associated with backup hardware, but increases the security of the data stored as the resources are all dedicated. This model is more expensive to provide than a Public Cloud because of the nature of the infrastructure and the provision of private networks for connectivity.

Public Cloud

A Public Cloud is where multiple organizations leverage the same Cloud Infrastructure as a Service. Unlike a Private Cloud, here the Cloud Infrastructure (whether a single system or partition) is shared by many organizations at the same time. The primary benefit of this approach is in cost savings, as cost versus the potential for impaired performance, since the resources are shared between multiple organizations.

In a DRaaS model, the issue when compared to the

Private Cloud is the perceived increase in security and compliance risk.

Choosing an HA/DR Provider

All DR Vendor Solutions Are Not Created Equal

Vendor DR solutions need to be evaluated holistically and the total cost of ownership of your DR agreement over the length of the term must be considered. IT must recognize the need to engage in a flexible partnership with a vendor where the IBM i infrastructure is scalable and will remain technologically compatible with your production environment.

1. Careful consideration must be given to understanding your service provider's IBM i capability and flexibility in providing the specific resources you require to fulfill the contract. Does the vendor have the prerequisite skills or is the vendor a broker outsourcing the entire service?

2. There must be a balance when a regional disaster strikes. Leading DR providers have the capability to balance the number of customers they service from each recovery site ensuring they do not oversubscribe their DR solution or staff resources. Consider whether

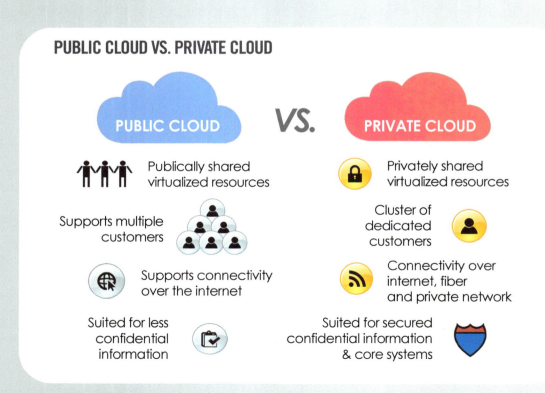

PUBLIC CLOUD VS. PRIVATE CLOUD

PUBLIC CLOUD VS. **PRIVATE CLOUD**

Publically shared virtualized resources

Supports multiple customers

Supports connectivity over the internet

Suited for less confidential information

Privately shared virtualized resources

Cluster of dedicated customers

Connectivity over internet, fiber and private network

Suited for secured confidential information & core systems

the vendor has a network of recovery sites from which to choose for regional diversity.

50%

of enterprises will have hybrid clouds by 2017

Source: Gartner

Traditional DR Hotsite Providers

Business executives must carefully evaluate their investments in recovery sites and related strategies so that their organizations do not fail during a disaster. Selecting a hotsite solution provider offers guaranteed emergency services in the event of natural, political, technological or regional disaster, or complete facility loss. Corporations contractually signed up for these programs will receive immediate priority for emergency server restoration services. The concept of a commercial hotsite was initially based on the idea that most organizations have a relatively similar set of IT infrastructure needs. In the event of a disaster, organizations would ship their backup tapes to the hotsite, get the operating system up and running, upload the backup information and continue to run the business.

A hotsite supports the restoration of critical business functions within the predetermined time and is backed by a service level agreement. A hotsite maintains a facility ready to assume processing responsibility immediately after the declaration of a disaster affecting the production system. Hotsites are comprised of all of the required server and data communication infrastructure, and sometimes DR staff resource necessary to meet your business requirements following any disaster event. Some hotsites are also fully equipped with workplace recovery services that also include desktop, telephony, fax machines and printing facilities all set up and waiting for you and your primary business users. Typically a hotsite service supports a critical business Recovery Time Objective (RTO) of getting all systems back up within a week, depending on recovery complexity.

When a disaster is declared, the customer's responsibility is to follow the DR plan, mobilizing staff and ensuring that the backup tapes and media are recovered from their secure offsite storage provider and delivered to the hotsite. Once delivered, the customer's IT DR team restores the backup tape data to the hotsite's server infrastructure and commences operations. Commercial hotsite vendors allow customers to use their facilities for a contracted number of weeks after a declared disaster. During this time, the customer must either restore back to the failed server, rebuild their data center or make alternative arrangements.

A commercial hotsite solution will have a number of recovery systems that are made available on a first-come, first-served basis for a tape recovery solution. If a customer organization owns a facility and manages all the IT resources at the hotsite, this facility is known as an internal hotsite. Such an arrangement ensures that the internal hotsite has dedicated all the resources required to ensure business continuity, to the customer organization. In addition, the hardware and software at the hotsite will be consistent with those in use at the production site. Many IT executives have realized that buying and managing the required critical Disaster Recovery equipment and building a facility in-house is significantly more expensive than the traditional approach of outsourcing Disaster Recovery to a hotsite. Commercial hotsite vendors distribute the high costs of technology and space among their many customers, versus the internal owned and operated solution costs being borne by one company.

Traditional on-premise DR strategies require changes in infrastructure to be accompanied by planning, budgeting and buying twice the required IT infrastructure capacity. It's clear that continuous improvement directly impacts capital expenditures for traditional Disaster Recovery planning.

Cost of Solution

The biggest barrier to implementing a solid Disaster Recovery foundation is the prohibitive cost of matching production hardware infrastructure components, i.e., a one-to-one system ratio. This capital expenditure can be difficult to justify. Even when the benefits are clear, these are expensive solutions for any business.

Infrastructure Complexity

The number of systems to provision can consume valuable recovery time. Options exist to optimize recovery time such as ensuring all maintenance procedures on production are duplicated for the DR environment, however this places a significant burden on IT and the application owners.

Reliability and Repeatability of Solution

Complex solutions are hard to test, primarily due to the difficulty of provisioning sufficient equipment to recreate all servers that need testing. Since complex solutions are difficult to test, they are typically not tested frequently - which should leave the business questioning the reliability of the solution.

Relying only on a traditional IBM i physical server recovery in a traditional hotsite can prove to be out-of-reach for many cost-constrained businesses. In many cases, it can lead a company to compromise on its disaster preparedness - a risky strategy. Instead, one can choose a DR solution where the costs of implementation and delivery efforts reflect the business value of the applications.

External Commercial Hotsites Compared to Internal Owned Hotsites

A balanced evaluation must relate directly to your organization's business needs. It may cost more to establish an internal hotsite due to the cost of acquiring an appropriate second site, equipment, networking, staffing, etc. However, the benefits derived from this solution and risk reduction may outweigh any additional cost over a commercial solution.

EXTERNAL VS. INTERNAL HOTSITE

External Commercial Hotsite	Internal Owned Hotsite
Lower total cost of ownership	Must own second, complete IT infrastructure
Costs shared between numerous clients	Total cost burden - capital
Technology upgrades supported	Upgraded technology must be purchased and aligned
Vendor's knowledge and expertise can be leveraged	Special training required
Risks related to shared use of equipment in a disaster	Risks related to equipment access in a disaster
Test time delay can be months	Available all the time
Declaration fees	No declaration fees
Multiple locations	Eggs all in one basket
Available staff support	You're on your own
Dedicated DR staff	Staff dedicated to regular IT functions
Specialist DR expertise available	General skills available only

Checklist for Selecting a Cloud Provider for Disaster Recovery

Today there are many companies that provide Cloud-based services covering a wide range of functionality. Looking at the Disaster Recovery Cloud market, what are the considerations to ensure the right choice for your organization?

Key Capabilities to Consider

- Does the service provider allow you, as customer, to define what constitutes a disaster?
- Is ample test time available (typically requiring less than three months' notice to the provider)?
- How much test time is included in the fixed cost? What is the cost for extra time?
- Does the provider have the requisite IBM i skills or are these outsourced?
- Are there any declaration and usage fees in a disaster scenario?
- Does the service provider offer multiple failover sites with regional or reasonable distance separation?
- Are low contention ratios ensured so you won't compete for server resources with other customers?
- Does the service provider perform application-level recovery on your behalf?
- Can the service provider demonstrate scalability to achieve near zero RPO and RTO?
- Are all of the above points demonstrated and supported by an SLA?
- Is the communication link between the DR Cloud Provider and your company's operational site sufficient to achieve the required RPO in normal operation? And if declaring a disaster, is it sufficient for your users to access their systems?
- Is the chosen DR solution infrastructure, under hardware and software maintenance, ensuring that operating system upgrades will mirror your company's production system requirements?

Security

- Does your industry dictate specific security standards for data and hosting thereof?
- Do you have Government contracts that dictate specific security regimes are adhered to? Make sure your chosen Cloud service provider can meet these security and regulation requirements.

- Is your chosen Cloud partner stable, and does the company have a solid industry track record?

- Is all or part of the service backed off to a third party? Do you know who this is? Does your contract clearly show an escalation path should that part of the service become unstable? Do a credit check, just like you would if you were taking on a new client.

Responsiveness

- Review a potential Cloud partner's initial response to your request and any ongoing communication and feedback. This is a potential partnership and partnerships fail if communication is lacking.

Organization

- Once you enter into an agreement, can you always find a responsible person to discuss any concerns with the service or are the layers of organization too deep? Are you confident that you have access to someone senior enough who will be an escalation point for your service if needed?

- Does the Cloud Provider offer a named account manager who will be your primary contact?

Data Center

- Has the data center been well thought out in its facilities, construction and location?

- Can you be sure it does not fall in a flood plain?

- Have other environmental risks been considered?

- Does the data center have any official accreditations?

- Does the physical security at the center protect your intellectual property?

- Is the integrity of the data center regularly tested?

These are important factors and if all have been considered should provide confidence that the service provider is serious about your data.

Take time to visit the data center facility if possible to get first-hand experience of the environment.

Service Management

- Does the Cloud partner have a detailed service level agreement (SLA) where their and your responsibilities are clearly defined?

Service management is one of the key aspects to delivering a first rate service and a clearly laid out SLA leaving little to interpretation is invaluable.

Testing

Your DRaaS solution hosted by the Cloud provider must be tested on a regular basis.

- Does the Cloud service provider offer regular testing time for you to test your Disaster Recovery plan so it can be validated?

- How much test time will be allocated to you and is this time detailed in the contract and SLA?

- What is the waiting time before you are allocated a test window?

- Is this a shared service?

- How many customers are competing for test time?

General

Don't underestimate the cost of changing providers and migrating your solution in the future, so spend the time on evaluating the service provider upfront to save time and effort in the future.

- Does the Cloud provider have the internal skills to manage the solution offered?

- Is this a company you are comfortable working with?

In addition, ensure your organization reviews and considers any contract language that governs accessibility, a la carte fees, test procedures, site fees, fee schedule, automatic triggers, and the scope of the equipment and related services that may be included or even excluded altogether. These can be overlooked when signing a contract only to catch you by surprise in the fine print and additional billing when you need the recovery provider the most.

Spend the time to go through a formal tender process. This way you will gather vital information on the industry and get a good feel for what a good service provider looks like. It can also help with any financial negotiations if you have costs and charges from multiple vendors.

CAN YOU PERSUADE YOUR BUSINESS TO INVEST IN HA/DR?

Building a business case for Disaster
Recovery investment

In order for any organization to build a Disaster Recovery plan, it must fully understand, both financially and strategically, what it stands to lose in the event of a disaster.

Disaster Recovery Objective Metrics

There are two major critical business considerations for a Disaster Recovery plan: the Recovery Time Objective (RTO) and the Recovery Point Objective (RPO).

The RTO is about DOWNTIME while the RPO is about DATA LOSS.

To understand your objectives for business continuity:

- How much downtime can your business afford before the impact is too great to recover from?
- How much data can be logistically and affordably recovered (or written off)?

Defining the business impact of these objectives is the first step of building the business case for a suitable Disaster Recovery solution for your organization.

Recovery Time Objective (RTO)

The Recovery Time Objective or RTO is the amount of downtime that an organization feels it can safely allow itself until operations resume. This period is measured from the moment the initial disaster is declared to the moment that critical business processes are available once more to users.

Recovery Point Objective (RPO)

The Recovery Point Objective or RPO is the acceptable amount of data measured in time that a business feels it can tolerate losing in a disaster. For example, how many hours of data can be either written off or manually recovered?

Your organization must determine the scope of data loss that can be tolerated; this can be defined by individual application or as a whole. Normally, the RPO is measured in terms of minutes to hours of lost data.

RECOVERY POINT OBJECTIVE (RPO) VS. RECOVERY TIME OBJECTIVE (RTO)

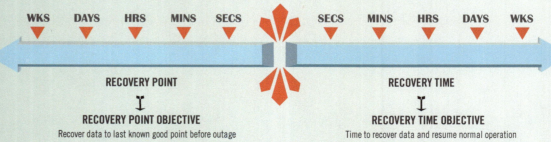

| WKS | DAYS | HRS | MINS | SECS | | SECS | MINS | HRS | DAYS | WKS |

RECOVERY POINT

RECOVERY POINT OBJECTIVE
Recover data to last known good point before outage

RECOVERY TIME

RECOVERY TIME OBJECTIVE
Time to recover data and resume normal operation

RECOVERY TIME
If failure occurs, how long can your business survive without data access?

RECOVERY POINT
How much data can you afford to lose?

When a massive failure takes down your data center at 3.00am on a long weekend, the declaration of a disaster and your response can be several hours later, which adds to your IBM i downtime.

If you define a Recovery Objective metric of 24x7x365, you're saying you can restore your infrastructure, applications and data to a point of 24 hours or better, and your business will be up and running within 36 hours of a disaster declaration. These metrics will help you determine if a tape-based recovery solution is suitable for your business, or if a real-time replication strategy will a better fit.

After determining the RTO and RPO of individual production IBM i LPARs (Logical Partitions), you can begin the process of determining which solution you'll need to implement to meet these business needs. Typically, the use of more than one type of DR solution is common to meet business requirements. This could lead to both hardware and software-based logical replication strategies being implemented in addition to traditional tape backup.

The Cost of DOWNTIME for Your Business

Downtime Is Costly To Your Business

When your IBM i server and mission-critical data is unavailable to your staff and customers for whatever reason, this is referred to as downtime. When unplanned downtime is experienced, your systems-based business processes will stop. When there is a stoppage of this nature to your business, it can get expensive very quickly.

Information Week quotes that the average downtime costs vary considerably across industries, from approximately $90,000 per hour in the media sector to a huge $6.48 million per hour for large online brokerages.

An online survey by CA Technologies and Coleman Parkes found that IT downtime costs businesses, collectively, more than 127 million person-hours per year, or an average of 545 person-hours per company, in employee productivity.

A conservative estimate from Gartner puts the hourly cost of downtime for computer networks at $42,000. So a company that suffers from worse-than-average downtime of 175 hours a year can lose more than $7 million per year. But the cost of each outage affects each company differently, so it's important to know how to calculate the precise financial impact.

A distinction does need to be made between planned downtime and unplanned downtime.

Unplanned downtime typically arises from some physical event, such as a server failure or environmental natural event causing site loss. In other words, a disaster and the recovery from that disaster together imply an extended period of time.

To estimate the cost of unplanned downtime of servers and applications to your business, you will need to take these factors into account:

- Total company revenue
- Employee productivity
- Income per transaction
- Lost sales opportunities; Lost inventory
- Lost customers and reputational damage
- Lost transactions
- Lost employee productivity

A simple way to calculate potential revenue losses during an outage is with this equation:

BUSINESS IMPACT CALCULATION OF DOWNTIME

DISRUPTION FREQUENCY × LIKELY DURATION × COST OF DOWNTIME = RISK COST

It is critical for a business to determine their maximum tolerance for downtime. When evaluating the causes of downtime it is best to take a worst case scenario. Consider your organization without access to your IBM i system in the middle of a busy day. It is important for IT groups to meet with the business groups so that both have input into the Disaster Recovery strategy. The following questions should be asked about downtime:

1. How many users will be affected in an outage?

2. What will be the impact on your customers?

3. Can you continue with manual processes if the systems are unavailable?

4. What is the maximum time your organization can be without access to the systems?

5. Can you calculate the cost of one hour's downtime in your organization?

POTENTIAL LOSS OF REVENUE CALCULATION

$$\text{LOST REVENUE} = (GR/TH) \times I \times H$$

GR = gross yearly revenue

TH = total yearly business hours

I = percentage impact

H = number of hours of outage

One of the Downtime Classics: The Story of Virgin Blue

Customers of Virgin Blue were really upset when they couldn't board their scheduled flights during an outage that lasted up to 11 long days. The outage fired up a lot of negative press as well as costing the company millions in profits.

In September 2010, Virgin Blue's airline's check-in and online booking systems went down. Virgin Blue suffered a systems failure on September 26 and a subsequent outage to the airline's internet booking, reservations, check-in and boarding systems. While the system recovery was completed within 21 hours, the business impact to Virgin Blue lasted for 11 days, affecting

around 50,000 passengers and 400 flights until service was back to normal on October 6.

The results: Virgin Blue's reservations management company, Navitaire, ended up compensating Virgin Blue for an amount speculated to be close to $15 million.

Virgin Blue's system outage nightmare

Planned Downtime

When you are building your business case for your HA/DR solution, you should take into account the key ROI that HA can offer organizations when it comes to planned downtime. HA gives you the freedom to perform potentially all the disruptive IT tasks (such as backups, ERP updates and operating system maintenance) with minimal or no impact on systems availability to the business and its customers.

Planned downtime is the outcome of maintenance that is disruptive to business operations. For example, on the IBM i, functionality on a production server or logical partition must be suspended while backups are taken. The business requires that backups are performed to protect its critical information, but increasingly, the business also requires the systems to be available to process orders. Hardware and software upgrades must be performed on a regular basis to ensure vendor compliance, but again, your business will not grant you the outage time required to obtain restricted state approval. These activities are usually scheduled and result in downtime for the system users typically measured in hours – which tends to be resisted by the business.

It's a fact that some organizations exclude planned downtime from their SLAs and systems availability time calculations, on the assumption that planned downtime has little or no relevance in this calculation nor financial impact upon the business user community. By excluding planned downtime, they can claim apparently high systems availability percentages or numbers of "nines". However, these figures do not represent reality.

Planned outages for IBM i servers account for nearly

90% of all recorded IT outages. Planned downtime is typically due to:

- Daily/weekly/monthly backup saves
- Software installation/upgrades (Application, Middleware)
- Server procedure updates and PTF installs
- Operating System upgrades
- Hardware or firmware upgrades

Take a look at the table below. The 26 days per year represents 7.12% of the time your IBM i is unavailable to your business. Holistically thinking, this is a direct impact to your systems availability uptime statistics. It means IT is only delivering 92.88% uptime to your business. If you know your business would consider this an IT failure, it becomes a significant business opportunity, and a critical aspect of your business case for HA/DR.

PLANNED DOWNTIME

	Per Week (Hours)	Per Year (Hours)
Weekly Backups	4	208
Daily Backups One Hour	7	364
Software Backups Yearly		28
Housekeeping System Maintenance		24
Total Planned Outages		624 hrs or 26 days

Source: IBM

This is the reason IT service delivery is deemed so expensive relative to return on investment. Examine the planned impact and ROI for High Availability. Calculate not just the cost of downtime, but *the opportunity for uptime*. In this illustrated scenario, your business can increase business productivity, reduce costs to the business, make your IT infrastructure more resilient, and most of all, remove risk from IT implementations.

Use This Method to Determine ROI:

1. Calculate your planned downtime using the table above

2. Note the total sum of the complete downtime in hours or days

3. Multiply this by the total number of days/hours by the cost of downtime per day to your business, as determined in the Potential Loss of Revenue calculation on the previous page: (GR/TH) x I x H. This is the financial benefit to your company of productivity improvements from your availability solution. This can be the justification for purchasing a High Availability solution, or increasing additional technology to further enhance your systems availability.

4. Compare these savings to the costs of the solution to calculate your ROI. The numbers bring a new realization to the benefits of looking at the big picture.

The Cost of DATA LOSS for Your Business

As with downtime, data loss is hugely damaging to a business. In the recent past it may have been acceptable to lose a day's data after a serious machine outage and it was not unusual for a business's Disaster Recovery strategy to be based solely on tape backups. Often the data could be manually re-created. This is no longer the case for most modern businesses as the volume of data changes has grown exponentially in the past 5 years and can no longer be easily recreated if lost. When preparing a Disaster Recovery strategy the IT and Business must agree on the size, scope and possible impact of data loss to the organization. The following questions must be answered:

1. What is the size of the database?

2. What volume of changes occur across the database over 24 hours?

3. Can data transactions be re-created if lost and if so will this contribute to overall downtime?

4. What would be the real effect to the business if up to 24 hours of data updates were lost?

BUSINESS IMPACT CALCULATION OF DATA LOSS

*Typically processed within the period specified

THE REAL COST OF UNPLANNED DOWNTIME

Did you know

it costs your business more than $11,000 per minute when your data center is down - according to a study by the Ponemon Institute...

...And

95% of respondents experienced one or more unplanned outages within the last two years!

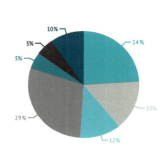

A Gartner study projected that "Through 2015, 80% of outages impacting mission-critical services will be caused by people and process issues, and more than 50% of those outages will be caused by change/configuration/release integration and hand-off issues." - Ronni J. Colville and George Spafford

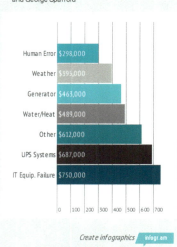

Create infographics

If an organization's Disaster Recovery strategy is based on daily tape backups then that organization has accepted the risk of up to 24 hours data loss. Most IBM i sites update between 3 and 40GB of data per day. Finding the answers to 1-4 above is essential in developing any Disaster Recovery strategy.

Return on Investment (ROI)

Return on investment for high availability is the value of an HA/DR solution compared to the costs of downtime without a solution. Simply determine the potential savings by calculating the costs of system and or application downtime compared to the cost of the HA/DR solution.

Cost Justification for Business Resiliency

HA and DR are being considered by many organizations today as a necessary combination to deliver true business resiliency. An HA solution on its own does not automatically support both Disaster Recovery and more importantly, systems availability. You must still employ tape backup practices, role swap procedure testing and Disaster Recovery planning. Disaster Recovery is a combination of how long you wait to bring your business back up (RTO) after a failure and, how available the systems are. The better you define this, the more demonstrable your ROI will be.

Today's HA solutions are much more than just IT insurance policies built strictly for Disaster Recovery. HA is now an ROI-generating investment by your organization that will add value to the business every day. HA solutions provide this value by enabling businesses to:

- Eliminate costs due to planned downtime
- Improve business productivity
- Sustain revenue growth and profitability
- Minimize risks by managing planned downtime
- Support unplanned downtime interruptions.

The last and most important consideration is to foster senior management's understanding and obtain agreement, using planned and unplanned downtime cost estimates. Businesses that must comply with regulatory standards such as Sarbanes-Oxley and HIPAA or their equivalent should automatically qualify for DR budget in order to meet these obligations.

Once you have established these three critical DR considerations - your budget, how quickly you need to recover key applications (RTO) and how much data you can afford to lose (RPO) - you can select the appropriate HA solution. At this point, with a detailed understanding of the business needs and expectations, you may discover that traditional tape backup won't be good enough to achieve your RTO and RPO goals for your most critical applications, nor the time lost to the business. Solutions vary, but you must consider your acceptable loss of data and acceptable length of system outage. Those combined should drive your availability investment. Keeping the business operational 365 days a year to support both disaster (unplanned) and IT operations (planned) outages is a good return that even your CFO will recognize.

An HA solution configured within an effective business continuity strategy will keep data and systems protected against extended outages, planned and unplanned, while also contributing to systems availability for day-to-day tasks when crises aren't looming.

Remember, your IBM i is always open for business, because your organization is always open for business, because your customers say so. When it comes to data protection and systems availability, hope is not a strategy; preparedness is.

Cost Considerations

When looking at the pricing models contrasting 'no action' with a Cloud-based DRaaS solution, a commercial or private hotsite, or against a customer-owned secondary system hosted in a second data center, a detailed cost analysis is required. Monthly subscription rates are not the only costs that need consideration.

Consider the following:

- Your monthly fee schedule
- Operating system upgrade costs on the DR system
- Additional third party service costs
- Disaster declaration fees
- Penalties for premature disaster declaration and subsequent cancellation
- Technical support fees
- Logistical tape-handling fees
- Bandwidth costs between the sites
- Cost for restoration back to a recovered production system
- Impact on the company's cash flow during the declaration and management of the disaster.

Are IT Deliverables aligned with Business Needs?

The scope of any Disaster Recovery solution should be driven by one key objective: the business must have access to all the critical systems and IT infrastructure required to conduct normal production activities, with minimal downtime and data loss. The acceptable downtime and data loss for each organization is defined by its Recovery Objectives.

Some of the typical oversights of a faulty DR plan are:

1. IT plans for best case instead of worst case for all aspects.

2. IT incorporates tape-based recovery with a reliance on staff to perform flawless execution under unrealistic disaster conditions.

3. IT doesn't take into account the realities of a regional disaster, in particular staff availability, access and loss of power.

4. While consideration is typically given to the recovery of data from an IT perspective (i.e., the technical process), consideration isn't given to when and how data is restored. It is critical that a business understands in advance of a disaster, the impact that a tape data restore will have on their business operations following restoration activities.

Clearly, businesses must align their data protection schemes operationally and strategically with their goals for Disaster Recovery and business continuity. They must also communicate their recovery objectives with all stakeholders who are becoming increasingly aware of the importance of protecting their business data, their most valuable business asset.

RTOs are moving from days to hours/minutes and to meet these, companies must consider data replication solutions that provide real-time protection of corporate data.

Alongside the importance of data is the importance of up-time. Organizations rely on technology to run their businesses, so downtime is a business issue. Data protection and high availability are related but still deliver distinctly different objectives. Maintaining continuous application availability is becoming essential to overall business continuity efforts as felt in a disaster. Businesses must set measurable goals for systems and data recovery times (RTOs and RPOs) based upon staff capabilities and current technologies and procedures.

Are your business needs and deliverables fully aligned? Take the test; go to maxava.com/disaster-recovery-scorecard. Then review it alongside your business colleagues to ensure you're on the same page. You need to think about:

- Minutes of tolerated downtime
- Number of transactions per hour
- Downtime cost per hour
- Acceptable financial loss
- Importance of corporate reputation
- Number and roles of users affected.

DECIDING YOUR DISASTER RECOVERY STRATEGY

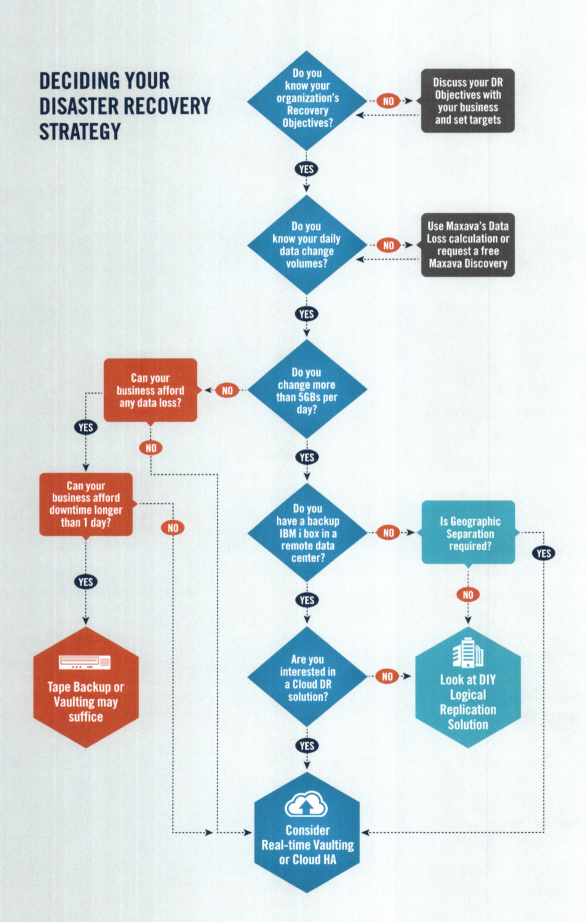

Do you know your organization's Recovery Objectives?
— NO → Discuss your DR Objectives with your business and set targets
— YES ↓

Do you know your daily data change volumes?
— NO → Use Maxava's Data Loss calculation or request a free Maxava Discovery
— YES ↓

Do you change more than 5GBs per day?
— NO → **Can your business afford any data loss?**
   — YES → **Can your business afford downtime longer than 1 day?**
      — YES → **Tape Backup or Vaulting may suffice**
   — NO →
— YES ↓

Do you have a backup IBM i box in a remote data center?
— NO → **Is Geographic Separation required?**
   — YES →
   — NO → **Look at DIY Logical Replication Solution**
— YES ↓

Are you interested in a Cloud DR solution?
— NO → **Look at DIY Logical Replication Solution**
— YES ↓

Consider Real-time Vaulting or Cloud HA

DR Strategy Checklist

The components of your business impact analysis and mission-critical server ranking will be used as the basis for the development and implementation of a supporting recovery strategy.

Ensure the following information is absolutely clear:

❒ The critical business processes have all been identified

❒ The availability and recovery requirements for these critical processes are identified

❒ The backup and recovery strategies reflect the assumed Disaster Recovery scenarios

❒ The availability and recovery strategies are scalable, flexible and compliant

❒ The assumptions behind each availability and recovery strategy are clearly stated

❒ The Recovery Timeframe Objectives (RTOs) for the critical processes are defined

❒ The Recovery Point Objectives (RPOs) for the critical processes are defined.

The DR planning team needs to examine the technology strategies available, to ensure their organization is successful if a recovery is required in a disaster. The appropriate technology solution supporting the recovery and availability strategies must meet the business objectives agreed in the initial analysis. This will include supporting procedures and effective DR planning, data backup requirements, offsite tape media storage, recovery restoration procedures, system redundancy, resiliency, network analysis and communications, infrastructure redundancy, replication software implementation and infrastructure review.

DR Strategy Challenges

The challenge in selecting DR solutions from an infrastructure standpoint is that there is a tendency to view the DR solutions as individual product technologies and piece together the total solution. Instead, DR solutions need to be viewed as a complete, integrated potentially multi-product solution.

For many organizations, the all-encompassing DR strategy is to simply back up everything to tape daily, send the tapes offsite, and rely on the historical uptime of the IBM i platform to guarantee that it will never go down. However, when a severe hardware failure does occur in the server, or a primary facility is damaged or totally lost, the 48 hours it takes to bring up the system and 24 hours minimal amount of data loss should be challenged by both IT and the business.

To identify recovery strategies, you should consider the immediate, short and long-term impact caused by the occurrence of a disaster. The question only remains whether the outage is an incident or a disaster. Strategies also differ on the basis of long-term and short-term recovery goals. You can adopt various strategies ranging from basic offsite tape storage to HA with multiple sites.

General Guidelines for Selecting Recovery Strategies

Disaster Recovery strategies are many and varied. Some organizations rely on daily tape backups, others have moved to offsite remote backups or vaulting while yet others have embraced real-time data replication and mirroring. Cost is obviously an important factor in choosing a strategy. Generally the higher the protection required, the more a strategy will cost.

If your organization cannot afford to invest in a high level data recovery strategy then you must accept some data loss and downtime as inevitable after a disaster. The Disaster Recovery strategy must be accepted by both IT and the business, and the risks must be well understood, signed off and accepted. Whereas decisions on recovery strategy were previously left to the IT department, these decisions are now increasingly made at Board level.

HA Delivers Value Over Traditional Tape Backups

- Tape backups can only restore data to the point of the last successful save

- RPO is significantly lower with HA (minutes versus hours to days)

- RTO is significantly lower with HA (minutes rather than days)

- Gartner reports over 20% of tape-based backups are either not completed, incomplete data sets, or un-usable - can you afford that risk?

- Eliminate planned outages for executing backups

- Store data offsite – generally outside the local region, out of harm's way.

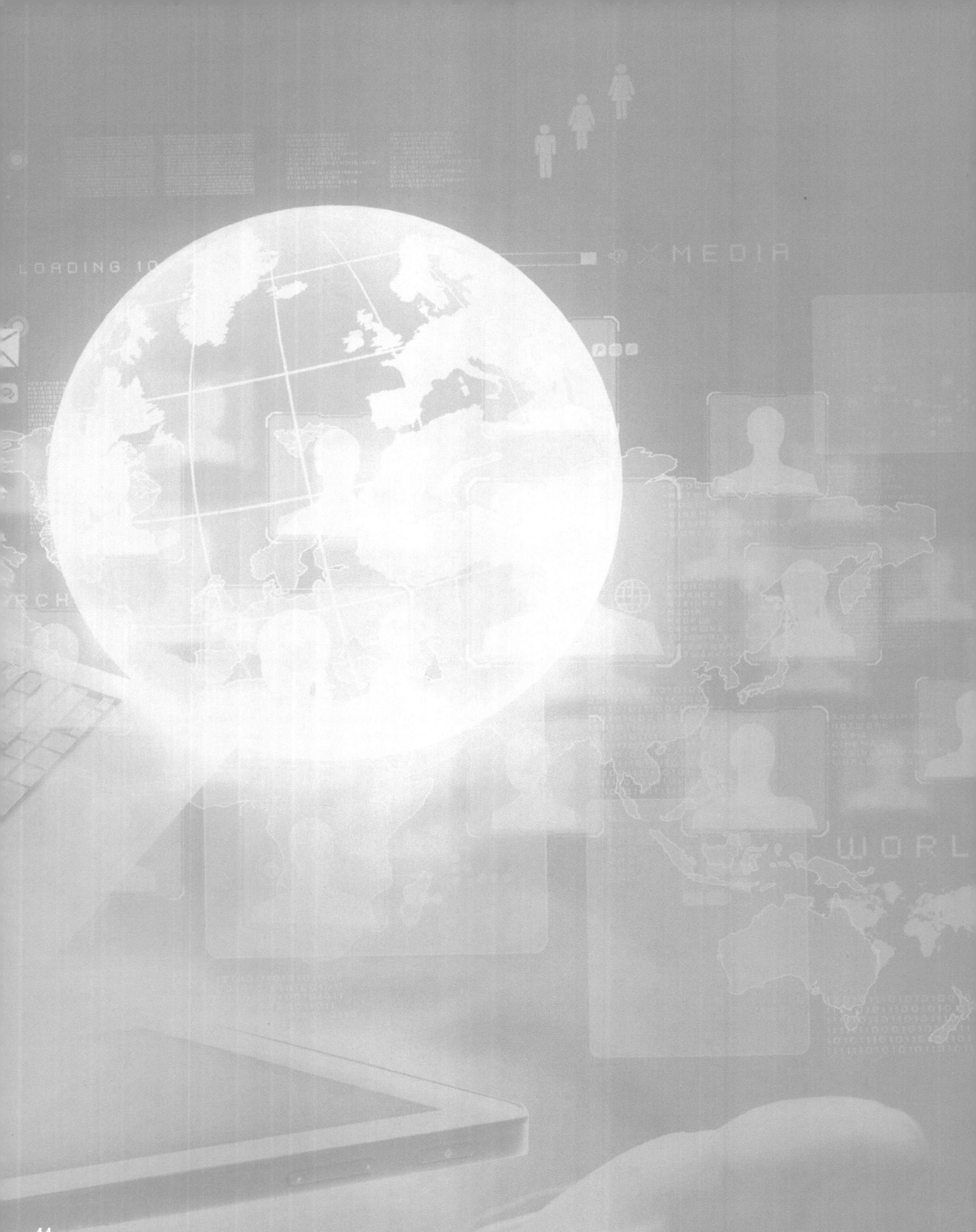
LOADING 10
MEDIA
WORL

MAXAVA SOLUTIONS
FOR HA/DR

Find out more about the unique features
of Maxava HA that can help you protect
your data and your business.

MAXAVA
MAXIMUM AVAILABILITY

Maxava has developed its own High Availability software for IBM i, 'Maxava HA', and has been servicing customers around the globe for over 15 years.

Maxava offers High Availability software that uses the full native functionality of the IBM i operating system, Remote Journaling. The Maxava HA suite provides real-time replication, virtually unlimited concurrent apply processes, constant data checking, an easy-to-use GUI and maxView, and Maxava HA's proprietary mobile monitoring system, Maxava Cloud Console (MCC).

Maxava can ensure data loss and downtime protection in any IBM i configuration: On-Premise, Hybrid or Cloud. It can replicate data and objects in real-time to any number of IBM i systems, regardless of location. Whether the backup server is in the same building, across town, interstate, or in another country, Maxava HA can replicate the database to a remote location of choice, ensuring complete data security.

An important point for future-proofing IT decisions is that Maxava HA can also support a move from any one of these configurations to another – and back. Organizations don't need to feel limited before they even get started, and can feel confident that these configuration changes are fully supported both technically and in the licensing model.

Maxava HA's features include:

- Unequalled performance
- Guaranteed implementation success
- Simple management in minutes per day
- 24x7x365 expert support

MAXAVA HA SUITE - SUPPORTED CONFIGURATIONS

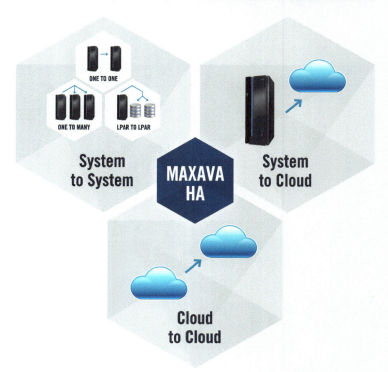

MAXAVA HA - UNDERLYING TECHNOLOGY

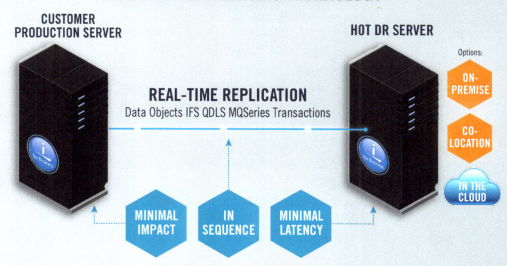

CUSTOMER PRODUCTION SERVER

HOT DR SERVER

Options:

ON-PREMISE

CO-LOCATION

IN THE CLOUD

REAL-TIME REPLICATION
Data Objects IFS QDLS MQSeries Transactions

MINIMAL IMPACT

IN SEQUENCE

MINIMAL LATENCY

- Local and mobile GUI interfaces

- Continuous software enhancement

- Honest and transparent pricing, upgrades and license transfers

- Remote monitoring and management

- Readiness testing: Role swap and virtual role swap

- Fully supported Cloud DR options.

Maxava Cloud Replication and Cloud Recovery Services

Maxava's architectural focus on producing the highest performing, fastest replicating software in the market, while maintaining the best operational efficiency and ease of use characteristics, ensures Maxava HA significantly leads the market in IBM i Cloud HA and DR. Over 7 years of experience in delivering real, live, production Cloud environments ensures that our software has been, and continues to be, tested in the real world on a daily basis.

Key features necessary for efficiency in high volume multi-tenanted environments, such as Simulated Role Swap™, in-built remote monitoring, mobile system access, command scripting functionality, multi-streamed replication for data, objects and IFS – and sheer replication speed – are delivered as standard with Maxava HA.

As noted in Chapter 3, the benefit of fully-hosted

Cloud services is that some of the fundamental HA/DR functions are removed from a business and provided as part of a "one-stop" solution based on clear contractual terms and agreed SLAs for an inclusive and predictable monthly fee.

Maxava offers either the full Cloud-hosted service, or alternatively the necessary components for a Cloud Service Provider ("CSP") to create its own "OEM" Cloud HA solution for IBM i. Either way, Maxava HA provides the best replication engine for IBM i with the right technical support and commercial terms to deliver a cost effective solution that meets both business partner and end customers' requirements.

The Cloud Infrastructure Model

In the IBM i environment Maxava delivers solutions for four of the seven components of the Cloud Infrastructure model:

- Facilities

- Technology

- Systems & Resiliency

- Processes

Maxava HA Software (including implementation services) sits within the "Systems & Resiliency" layer as it operates at the operating system level.

With provision of Monitoring Services for Maxava HA software, Maxava also operates at the "Processes" layer.

Maxava Cloud Infrastructure Model

▶ **STRATEGY AND VISION**

▶ **ORGANIZATION**

▶ **PROCESSES** (application and HA, monitoring and management) — MAXAVA

▶ **APPLICATION** (ERP, etc)

▶ **SYSTEMS & RESILIENCY** (operating systems and HA applications) — MAXAVA

▶ **TECHNOLOGY** (Power Systems, networking equipment, etc) — MAXAVA

▶ **FACILITIES** (data center, redundant power, comms etc) — MAXAVA

In addition, Maxava-provided Cloud Services also meet "Facilities" and "Technology" requirements for end customers by providing hosted systems for backup and recovery services. The Maxava-provided data center environment is made available through contracted co-location services.

Maxava works with specialist partners who provide solution offerings in the areas of "Applications", "Organization" and operational "Strategy and Vision".

Maxava Cloud Replication & Cloud Recovery Services

Maxava has two major Cloud Service offerings;

1. Disaster Recovery as a Service (DRaaS)
2. Real-Time Vaulting (DRaaS-RTV)

Maxava DRaaS

Businesses purchasing Maxava DRaaS receive the following features:

- Full replication to the Maxava Cloud IBM i using Maxava HA Enterprise+ software

- Full monitoring of HA environment

- Customer monitoring of HA environment in real-time via iPhone, etc.

- Management of HA environment and HA/DR system

- Full and Simulated Role Swap™ testing of IBM i system as required (1xSRS per year included)

- Guaranteed contracted resource availability in event of a disaster

- Additional resource provision based on availability at time of disaster

- Client supported failover by Maxava during a disaster declaration (included)

- Ability to role swap back to production system once disaster situation is resolved

- Target time for role swap to fully active backup in event of disaster declaration is measured in minutes

- Standard set of most common IBM i program licensed products included

- The Maxava Cloud provides network equipment to establish a Site-to-Site VPN connection.

Additional third-party resources (additional software licenses, etc.) necessary are chargeable to end customer's account.

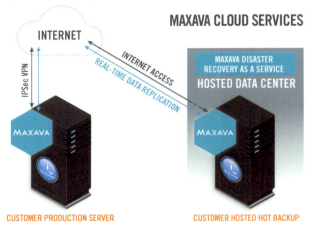

MAXAVA CLOUD SERVICES

INTERNET

INTERNET ACCESS

REAL-TIME DATA REPLICATION

IPSec VPN

MAXAVA DISASTER RECOVERY AS A SERVICE

HOSTED DATA CENTER

CUSTOMER PRODUCTION SERVER

CUSTOMER HOSTED HOT BACKUP

Maxava DRaaS-RTV

Businesses purchasing Maxava DRaaS-RTV receive the following features:

- Full replication to the Maxava Cloud IBM i using Maxava HA Enterprise⁺ software

- Full monitoring of HA environment

- Management of HA environment and HA/DR system

- Maxava will facilitate the supply of standby IBM i hardware in the event of disaster, subject to availabiltiy

- At the time of disaster, a recovery copy of replicated data and objects will be provided on tape and dispatched within 24 hours

- Disaster declaration support by Maxava staff (chargeable).

Any additional third-party resources (additional software licenses, etc.) necessary would be chargeable.

Maxava Cloud Monitoring and Management

Businesses who replicate their data to Maxava's Cloud IBM i systems around the world are fully monitored and managed by a team of Maxava specialists. Monitoring is delivered on a 24x7x365 basis. Businesses running Maxava solutions on their own infrastructure can also be managed and monitored by Maxava. This is a very useful service for those who don't have the required resources to devote to their own monitoring and management. It ensures that their systems are always replicating data, and are ready to respond to any disaster situation when required.

The Maxava Cloud Console (MCC) utilizes health-check data sent by the user's IBM i system to determine replication and basic system alert status based on pre-agreed threshold settings. MCC gathers relevant replication status information as well as general system statistics and passes this to Maxava's secure Cloud monitoring server. Alerts are then relayed to pre-specified personnel via a browser-based interface and via email and Twitter.

The monitoring tool also offers the ability to perform a role swap on command from a mobile device or browser, remotely accessing Maxava's proprietary command scripting functionality. In the event of a failure, Maxava customers can simply activate a failover to the backup server.

Testing in a Maxava Cloud Environment

Testing is critical to ensure that user data and application objects are securely captured, transported and applied to the backup server in the event of emergency downtime. Amongst other things, testing ensures that new computers, applications and processes have been taken into account in the backup function. However most HA/DR solutions require the business to take down the production server for testing. As a result, IT specialists are often reluctant to run tests as regularly as they should – and some never get to run them at all.

Maxava's Simulated Role Swap™ feature lets businesses test their Disaster Recovery process without downtime. Simulated Role Swap™ temporarily turns the backup system into a simulated primary system for testing purposes, leaving the primary system live and unaffected. The business can then run the test to ensure that when it really matters, everything will work.

maxava.com/simulated-role-swap

NOW WHAT?

The next steps to start protecting
your data and your business.

MAXAVA
MAXIMUM AVAILABILITY

"ABOVE
ALL, BEING
PREPARED IS
ONE OF THE
GREATEST
INVESTMENTS
YOU CAN
MAKE."

You've learned all about the evolution of Disaster Recovery, how disasters of various types can impact business, and the strategies you can employ to minimize the risk of impact to your business.

You've also read about the critical importance of fully understanding the risks to your business. Without this understanding you cannot hope to prepare an adequate DR plan, nor can you achieve an appropriate level of investment from the business. Your executives must fully comprehend the potential impact of any downtime, before they can be expected to buy into a suitable protection strategy.

Comprehensive business continuity planning will ensure your organization is equipped to withstand a raft of human or natural disasters. Above all, being prepared is one of the greatest investments you can make: investigating the considerations around specific service providers, Cloud enablement or a more traditional software-based approach, testing your plan, and planning for a crisis.

Tools to Help You Move Forward

If you're thinking seriously about an investment in Disaster Recovery, you can very easily start the process right away. One or both options below will help you take the next steps towards protecting your business data, and your business.

- Request a free assessment or 'Discovery' report of your environment today.

- Initiate a Request for Proposal from your supplier.

Discovery

Maxava can provide you with a free, no obligation IBM i System Discovery Report. Maxava runs the Discovery program across your environment without impacting your day-to-day operations. The tool gathers information about your system setup and no actual customer data. Information is collated such as i5/OS version, ASP configuration, total storage, number and size of libraries, number of objects, IFS volumes and the current journal configuration you have in place (if any). The report is generated on your system, and once verified Maxava will provide you with a Discovery Report outlining your physical environment. This document can be used as an important building block to your future Disaster Recovery plans, including telling you the bandwidth speed you'll need to meet your recovery objectives.

To initiate a discovery request for your site go to maxava.com/discovery and fill in your details.

Build a Request for Proposal

Maxava has created an online tool specifically designed for the IBM i platform, that allows you to build and customize an independent document setting out the potential requirements for your High Availability/Disaster Recovery solution. You'll generate your own PDF document that can be distributed to HA/DR vendors.

To initiate the process for a professional quality HA RFP in minutes, go to haproposalgenerator.com

Advice Note and Disclaimer

The information contained in the Maxava Disaster Recovery Strategy Guide is intended for general information purposes only, and by its nature should not be considered comprehensive or used in place of a system audit, consultation or advice from Maxava and/or your specialist IT provider. Maxava recommends that all decisions regarding DR solutions be made by/with the assistance of a qualified DR expert who can evaluate your specific environment and requirements. This guide does not constitute advice on your specific requirements, and the guide does not make representations or warranties of any kind.

If you have any questions about the information in the guide, please call Maxava or your specialist IT provider.

Further Resources

For up to date resources go to:
maxava.com/drguide-resources

Resources Include:

- Technical Addendum – For a deeper dive on a more technical level

- Jargon Buster - A dictionary of common HA/DR terms

- Maxava Overview video – Learn more about Maxava HA

- Simulated Role Swap™ video – Discover how to test your DR without downtime

- maxView lite – Download a free copy of our IBM i remote monitoring tool

- Request for Proposal (RFP) Online tool – Create a professional quality HA RFP in minutes

www.ingramcontent.com/pod-product-compliance
Lightning Source LLC
Chambersburg PA
CBHW041428050326
40689CB00003B/704